A Golden Treasury of Prayers

A Golden Treasury of Prayers

Canon Francis J Ripley

GRACEWING

First published 1989 by Print Origination, Liverpool

Reprinted 2014
by
Gracewing
2 Southern Avenue
Leominster
Herefordshire HR6 0QF
www.gracewing.co.uk

ISBN 978 0 85244 858 8

Cover design by Bernardita Peña Hurtado

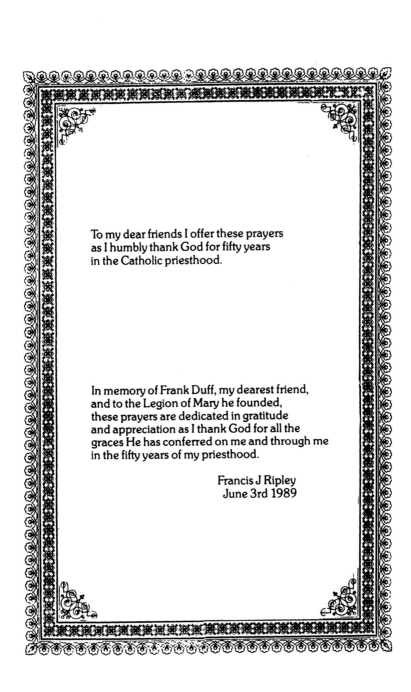

To my dear friends I offer these prayers
as I humbly thank God for fifty years
in the Catholic priesthood.

In memory of Frank Duff, my dearest friend,
and to the Legion of Mary he founded,
these prayers are dedicated in gratitude
and appreciation as I thank God for all the
graces He has conferred on me and through me
in the fifty years of my priesthood.

Francis J Ripley
June 3rd 1989

1   MARY MOTHER

How wonderful it is to begin the New Year
with you, my dear Mother Mary.
Mother of God! The dignity is incomprehensible.
The human mind cannot comprehend God's infinity.
Yet you, Mother, are really and truly Mother of the Infinite.
Therefore I can never honour you as your dignity deserves.
You became God's Mother when you said
"Behold the Handmaid of the Lord;
Be it done to me according to your word." (Luke 1,38).
We can never repay you for your obedience
and submission to God's will.
It was that which made the Incarnation possible,
and salvation and the Church
and all that the Church has meant to humanity.
O Mother, humanity needs you now.
Pray for us.
Pray that people everywhere will accept your Son.
Pray for poor pagans who have never heard of Him.
Pray for your second child, the Church.
Pray that she will grow in zeal.
Pray that more men and women everywhere
will give themselves to the priesthood and religious life.
Pray, dear Mother, for the Pope, bishops, priests and religious.
The Church needs a vast renewal of spirit.
She needs renewed apostolic zeal.
She needs a return to the spirit of the early centuries
when nothing was so important as the conversion of souls.
She needs to review her priorities
to restore the priority of the spiritual.
She needs a renewed faith in herself.
She needs to see herself as she really is,
the one and only society on earth
founded and given her constitution by your divine Son.
Pray, blessed Mother, that the Church will purify herself.
Pray that she will return to the simplicity of the Gospel.
Pray for your children that some of them at least
will be the Saints the Church needs
more than anything else.
O blessed Mother, you know the Church's needs better than I do.
Pray, pray that they will be fulfilled.

2 THE CHURCH

O Jesus, I can never thank You enough for your Church.
Nor can I ever hope to thank You for giving me the Church to be
 my mother.
Give me the grace to value her as I should
and always to be loyal to her and
to love her with true filial love.
In the Church You remain with us.
If You had just left us an organisation
to teach, lead and guide us with your authority
we could never adequately thank You.
But you have made your Church a living organism,
pulsating with your own divine life,
living and moving,
teaching and sanctifying,
ruling and forgiving
as You did when you walked on earth.
By her inmost life,
animated by your Holy Spirit,
the Church is our divine guide, our shepherd, our teacher.
You gave life to your Church when You died on the cross.
She came forth from your side on Calvary.
Like your Blessed Mother, a new Eve,
mother of all the living.
You sanctified her, Lord,
by shedding your Precious Blood for her.
You gave her your very own power.
You made her your spouse.
Through her, You, O Lord,
will continue your work
of making us holy and directing us.
Lord, help me to understand all this.
Convince me so that the truth will dominate
all my thoughts, words and deeds.
All around me the Church is regarded more and more
as a merely natural organisation.
Men without faith speak and write about her in this way.
Misunderstanding her inner nature
they lead others to error with them.
Dear Lord, strengthen your Church every day.
Make her be seen as your living other self.

3 THE BODY OF CHRIST

Lord Jesus, enliven my faith in your Church.
I know, I believe most firmly that You are the living Head of
the Church.
You rule her invisibly by your Spirit,
the Holy Spirit who is the Church's soul.
Ceaselessly You sustain your Church.
You give her life.
You give grace to each of her members.
She lives by You alone
unique in the entire world.
She is holy with your holiness;
through her loving union with You.
She is the mother of souls.
She is a prolongation of your divine self.
Dear Master, may all peoples be convinced of this.
May they see in your Church a living organism
sustained by You in a superhuman divine way.
In the Holy Eucharist we unite ourselves with You
and are nourished by your immaculate flesh.
So through the Church we are guided by You,
ruled by You, made alive by your grace,
nourished by your doctrine.
Lord, I pray that people everywhere will learn
that they can have no greater assurance of living by your Spirit
of being taught by You
and directed by You
than by uniting themselves to the Church
and joyfully and faithfully
lovingly and loyally following her directives.
Good Master, inspire the people of this world
to realise all these wonderful truths.
I sorrow, sweet Jesus, when I hear your Church
discussed and described
just as if she is no more than a worldly organisation
that must fit in and change according to the moods of the times.
Too often expediency replaces truth,
the easy way of least resistance the narrow path of the Cross,
so that the truly divine nature
of your spouse and our mother is forgotten.
O Lord, I pray make all men understand the simple truth
that the Church is your Body.

4   THE BISHOPS

Lord Jesus, You have given us bishops,
successors of your Apostles
to rule and guide and care for your Church.
Make them all men of courage, truth and love.
I believe that your Church, your mystical Body,
is your other self.
It is one,
ruled by the successor of St. Peter,
the Pope, the bishop of Rome.
Those who reject the authority of Peter
cannot be members of your Church.
Enlighten our bishops to understand in faith.
Make them realise with deep, sincere conviction
that unity among your followers
must be the unity You desire,
unity in the whole truth.
Guide them never to sacrifice the whole truth
about any doctrine
on the plea that it will lead our separated brethren to You.
Bring your infinite power and love to bear
that scandal will not be caused by false irenicism.
Guide all your bishops.
Keep them loyal to your whole truth.
Never allow any one of them to raise false hopes.
Never allow any one of them to compromise or dilute truth.
Move those who have left us,
the sheep without a shepherd,
to seek You in all the fullness of your truth.
Lord, flood the hearts and minds of all your bishops
with effective evangelical zeal.
Give them the fullness of faith and trust,
animated by charity,
firm and immovable as a rock,
courageous, enlightened faith
to which it is given to conquer the whole world.
Make every one of your bishops a leader of men.
Give them the guidance and help they need
to inspire their priests to be
zealous, gentle, loving and understanding.

5 A CHILD OF THE CHURCH

Lord, strengthen my faith in your Church.
I believe with all my heart
that there is nothing more glorious,
nothing more noble,
nothing more honourable
than membership of the one and only Church
which You founded.
I firmly believe that my membership of the Church
has hade me a member of your very own mystical Body
to be guided by You, O Jesus,
the one, sublime, infinite Head of the Body,
to be filled with the one and only divine Holy Spirit.
I believe that as a child of your Church
I am nourished during my exile on earth
with one doctrine and one same heavenly Bread.
I am convinced, Lord, and I wish all people were convinced
that, as St. Cyprian said, "He who does not have the Church for
a mother cannot have God for a father."
Lord, pour forth your saving grace in torrents
so that the human beings your love brought out of nothing
will know that You wish to sanctify and save them all
and that You wish to do it through your Church.
You know, dear Lord, how I believe that You gave your life
and shed your Blood for us.
You put your precious merits at our disposal.
You gave us Yourself in the Holy Eucharist.
You left us the heritage of your doctrine.
Give more people the grace to come to believe
that You wish the Church to be the one and only depository
and dispenser of these inestimable benefits.
Cause all members of your Church
to value and appreciate her as they should.
Convince them that it is to the Church they must go
with the complete confidence of children
to find You in her.
Make their love of the Church strong.
Make them have recourse to her with confidence.
In a word, Lord, give them the deep conviction
that devotion to the Church is devotion to You.

6   LOVE THE CHURCH

Lord Jesus, You are all powerful.
You willed in your infinite love
to make the Church your other self.
Hear me to-day as I make my own the words of an ancient Liturgy.
You have transmitted to the Church
the sovereign power You received.
By virtue of your dignity You make your Church Queen and Spouse.
You have given your Church power over the whole universe.
You told your Church that whoever hears her hears You.
Lord, use your infinite power and love and wisdom
to convince the world of this truth.
On earth You raised the dead to life.
Now, bring all to believe in the universal authority of your Church.
Give a special insight to penetrate and understand
all the implications of your words,
"Whatever you bind on earth shall be bound in heaven" (Matt. 18,18).
And "He who hears you, hears Me" (Luke 10,16).
Enliven my conviction that when You said these things
You conveyed to the Church your very own supreme authority.
Lord, pour graces into every mind and heart
to see your Church as the city seated on a hill.
Our poor human race so needs You.
It cannot find You while it rejects your Church.
Lord, guide your Church to speak and teach like You
with your love and your wisdom
in the way You taught, "as one having power" (Matt. 7,29).
the truths You most want men to learn.
Do not allow the leaders of your Church, O Lord,
to be side-tracked into emphasising secondary truths
at the expense of those which are basic
and most necessary for salvation.
Eternal King of souls, I beg of You to
stretch your omnipotent hand over your Church,
in Rome and in every part of the world
so that her children will be loyal, loving and obedient.
May your Church always remain pure and loving,
always and everywhere your Way, your Truth and your Life.
Defend her, omnipotent loving Lord; guard and guide her.
Lead her always along the straight and narrow way,
never the way of expediency, always the way of the Cross.

7 FAITH IN THE HOLY EUCHARIST

Lord Jesus, increase my faith
in both the reality and the significance
of your sacramental presence among us.
I believe that in Holy Mass
You have entrusted to your Church
a memorial of your death and resurrection,
a sacrament of love,
a sign of unity,
a bond of peace
and a pledge of eternal glory.
I believe that Holy Mass
is at one and the same time and inseparably
a sacrifice,
in which the sacrifice of the Cross is perpetuated,
a memorial of your death and resurrection
and a sacred banquet
in which the People of God share the benefits
of the sacrifice of redemption.
I believe that in the holy sacrifice
You, Jesus, offer Yourself to the Father through the priest.
I believe that his action is your action,
in Yourself and in your other self, your Church.
Lord make me worthy to participate in this sublime act every day.
Give me a real longing to identify myself with your Person,
your mission to souls,
your very condition of living.
Lord, I believe that nothing less
than the worship due to You, the one true God,
is due to You present before us in the monstrance.
I believe that You are present here by transubstantiation
and that the mystery of your eucharistic presence
is the centre of the whole life of the Church.
Lord, I long to lead souls to your altar,
to promote devotion to your presence
in every possible way.
I consecrate myself to You.
I renew the total gift of myself to You.
May I always respond in a way pleasing to You
to your infinite love of me.

8 ABANDONMENT

Once again, Lord, I profess my faith.
You are indeed Lord, Master of all creation.
Help me at all times to be faithful to the order You have established.
Your power overshadows me at every moment.
You are everywhere.
Your love is everywhere.
Your care for us as a Father who never rests.
As your loving child I want to do your will always.
I know, dear Lord, that I shall not always understand it.
Yet I want to obey because your will
is the will of infinite love, power, wisdom and goodness.
Help me, Father, to ask at every moment,
"Lord, what will You have me to do?"
I want to choose only what I believe is your will.
Strengthen my conviction that the only way to solid peace
is the way of submission.
May I always will what You will for me, Lord.
May I always seek for your working
beneath external appearances in people, in events, in circumstances.
Help me, Lord, to realise that You are acting upon me
at every moment,
putting before me things of infinite value.
I wish to use them to prove my faith, my hope and my love.
May I never forget, dear Lord, that in the main events of life
You make yourself known as adorably as You did
in the main events of Scripture or history.
You write your will on my heart
through the ordinary happenings of life.
You come to me, indeed, in the ordinary events of my daily life.
May I always remember that You, O God,
are infinite Wisdom and infinite Goodness and
that what You send to me at any moment must be most useful.
You intend it specially for me.
Each moment is the ambassador of your love.
Help me, O loving Father, to abandon myself to your will.
Help me to grow in faith, hope and love.
I know that then I shall be guided by You always.
Then I shall soar above despondency, dryness, illness,
suspicion, jealousy, prejudice and all the devil's snares.
Yes, Lord, give me the grace to abandon myself wholly to your will.

9   GRACE: DIVINE SONSHIP

Lord Jesus, to Nicodemus You said,
"Unless a man be born again, he cannot enter the kingdom of heaven."
St. Paul wrote to Titus about the cleansing power
"which give us new birth . . . . to become heirs" (Tit. 3,7).
How can I thank You, Lord, for making me your child
  through baptism?
You have renewed me in a way beyond nature.
You have invested me with new life.
You have brought the Holy Trinity to live within me.
Yes, Lord, I believe that I have received the Spirit of adoption
which makes me cry out "Abba, Father" (Rom. 8,15).
Your Holy Spirit Himself assures my spirit
that I am really your child, your heir
sharing your inheritance (ibid. 8,16).
Dear Father, when I think of your infinite attributes and perfections
I find it breathtaking to be really your son and heir
sharing the inheritance of your only-begotten Son.
O eternal Trinity, how sublime is this truth!
You come to live within me.
You bring me the new life which makes me
a partaker of the divine nature, your nature.
I believe with St. Paul that You, eternal Father,
chose me in Christ before the foundation of the world
to be a saint,
to be your adopted child through Jesus Christ (Eph. 1, 4-7).
You are so good that You have placed me spiritually in Christ
as I am naturally in the atmosphere which sustains me.
I know, I believe most firmly
that I cannot live spiritually apart from Jesus.
He is the source of all grace, all holiness.
I long to be able to say truly from the depth of my being,
"I live, now not I, but Christ lives in me" (Gal. 2,20).
Your love is only satisfied when I am taken into your divine family.
Your death, Jesus, made it possible for me
to be a new creature, the eternal Trinity's own child,
with a life far surpassing that of nature.
Give me your actual graces
to live according to what I have become,
clothed with a new self,
"born in Christ Jesus, a new creation" (2 Cor. 5,17).

10 DIVINE ADOPTION

Lord, I can never contemplate sufficiently
the truth that all who are baptised are really your children.
You have made me your child.
That is your free gift to me
but it is your love that makes You adopt me.
I recall the words of the Beloved Disciple,
"See how the Father has shown his love towards us,
that we should be counted as God's sons,
should be his sons.
We are sons of God even now . . . .
When He comes we shall be like Him;
we shall see Him then as He is.
Now a man who rests these hopes in him
lives a life of holiness; he, too, is holy" (1 John 1-3).
Lord, help me to comprehend the wonder of this truth.
How good You are to choose me,
to give me a new spiritual birth,
to adopt me,
to make me a co-heir with your only begotten Sopn.
May I never forget, loving Father, that as long as I die in your grace,
I shall see You, not in a mirror, but face to face.
Give me your grace constantly to begin this new life now,
to be your faithful child, in every sense like Jesus.
I resolve, with your help, that my spiritual life
will always be a relationship of real, chidlike love.
I am your adopted son, dear heavenly Father.
Earthly adoption does not give a share in the physical life of those
 who adopt
but You, Father, in adopting me make me really share your life.
In me you place a created miniature of your own divine nature.
Your Holy Spirit disposes me to cry out to You as my Father.
Strengthen my faith so that I shall accept your word as a loving child.
Strengthen my hope to accept your promises as a little child.
Enliven my charity to be the loving tenderness of a devoted child.
How wonderful it is to be adopted into your family, O God.
May I never forget that your will is the will of a loving Father.
Your divine Providence is the guidance of my tremendous Lover.
Give me, Lord, humility, trust, self-surrender, immolation, victimhood.
May I see everything in the context of your real fatherly love.
May the thought of your love dominate me as the sun dominates
 the firmament.

11   THE BLESSED TRINITY

I profess my faith today and say
"Blessed are the Holy Trinity and undivided Christ."
O God, how wonderful is your name in all the earth.
How can I ever comprehend the depths of the riches
of the wisdom of the knowledge of God (Rom. 11,33).
I adore you, God the Father of heaven.
I adore you, God the Son, Redeemer of the world.
I adore you, God the Holy Spirit, our Sanctifier.
I adore you, Father, from whom are all things.
I adore you, God the Son, through whom are all things.
I adore you, God the Holy Spirit, in whom are all things.
I profess my belief that uncreated is the Father
uncreated the Son, uncreated the Holy Spirit.
Infinite is the Father, infinite the Son, infinite the Holy Spirit.
Eternal is the Father, eternal the Son, eternal the Holy Spirit.
With the ancient Fathers I affirm my belief that
in the Blessed Trinity there is no before or after,
no greater or lesser,
but all three Persons are equally eternal with each other
and fully equal.
I worship in all things unity in the Trinity
and Trinity in the unity.
O blessed Trinity, I believe that You lived in an eternity
before you began to create anything.
For an eternity you were by Yourself and nothing else but You.
For that eternity, You, O God, were infinite in your activity.
For endless ages You rejoiced in the knowledge of Yourself
and in knowing Yourself.
You declared and expressed your knowledge in the infinite Word
your only begotten Son
to whom you communicated your nature, your life, your perfections.
Father and Son, You loved one another with an infinite love
and from your eternal mutual embrace
burst forth, without beginning, the Holy Spirit.
O God, I adore your eternal, essential activity within Yourself,
your infinite eternal knowing and loving, your very nature.
I thank you for allowing me to share in your nature,
in the very source of the divine Processions,
by which You are always eternally three Persons in one nature.
This I believe is the true fruit of baptism
when I was born again to a new, supernatural life.

12   HELL

My dear God, I thank you for revealing the truth about hell.
Grant that I may never forget it.
At every moment you offer me graces
to sanctify and save myself.
I believe—but help me to believe more vividly—
that if I do not use the graces You offer me
I could be separated from You forever.
Lord, I cannot imagine strongly enough what my state of mind
 would be
if I had to realise that I had lost You forever
and through my own fault.
Fill me now with a vivid realisation of your infinite perfection—
your love, your goodness, your wisdom, your beauty.
Inspire me to realise how terrible the remorse would be
if through my deliberate sin I had
to live a dark death,
tormented by the undying worm of conscience.
Lord, I have often thought about the fire of hell.
When you, Jesus, were warning us about eternal punishment
You chose to use the word "fire"
in preference to all the other words You might have used.
How terrible is that eternal fire,
darkness not light,
torturing body and soul,
angels as well as men.
Lord, I pray You, help me to realise
that in your love and mercy You created it
as a fitting punishment for sin.
But, Lord, even greater than the power of fire in hell
is the pain of loss.
May I never have to endure it.
Make my sense of your love more compelling than ever.
You, good Lord, are no pitiless judge.
To save me from hell your only begotten Son died for me.
You could not have done more
to keep me safe from eternal torment.
Be with me now by your grace
at every step on my pilgrim way.
Never allow me to forget the reality and horror of hell.
May the very thought of it lead me to love You more.

13 HEAVEN

I pray today in the words of Solomon,
"Hear my prayers and the prayers of your people, Lord.
In your home in heaven hear us and forgive us" (I Kings 8,30).
I profess my faith: "Christ did not go into a man-made holy palace
which was a copy of the real one.
He went into heaven itself,
where He now appears on our behalf in the presence of God"
 (Heb. 8,24).
I profess my faith: "Their angels in heaven I tell you
are always in the presence of my Father in heaven" (Matt. 18,10).
With the inspired writer I look forward to heaven.
"The city of the living God, the heavenly Jerusalem,
with its thousands of angels . . . .
the joyful gathering of God's first-born sons . . . .
the spirits of good people made perfect" (Heb. 13,23).
Lord, may I realise fully the sayings of Jesus,
"There will be more joy in heaven
over one sinner who repents . . . .
The angels of God rejoice
over one sinner who repents" (Luke 15, 7,50).
Lord, I pray that when you call me
I shall still be faithfully in your service and hereafter
enjoy rest in your presence (Apoc. 14,10).
May I never forget the blessings you keep for your people.
Grant that at every moment I may live so as to
possess with Christ what you have kept for me.
I offer all I suffer in any way during my life
in union with the sufferings of Christ.
I believe that if I share his sufferings
I shall also share his glory (Rom. 8,17).
With St. Paul I sigh, for so great is my longing,
for the house You have for me in heaven,
the home that You Yourself have made
which will last forever (2 Cor. 5,2).
No eye has seen, no ear has heard
the consummation of your wisdom, loving Father,
things beyond the power of human comprehension
that You have prepared for those who love You (1 Cor. 2, 7-10).
Lord, grant that I may always remember these things,
always look forward to possessing the blessings
You keep for your faithful lovers in heaven (1 Peter 1,4).

My God, Father, Son and Holy Spirit, you live in me always.
When the water of baptism fell on me
You took up your abode within me.
Make your presence stronger;
make your affection ever more intimate;
make your friendship ever deeper.
I know I depend entirely on your grace.
Therefore I impore you to help me advance in charity.
Keep coming to me, O Blessed Trinity.
Reveal Yourselves to me ever more vividly.
My Jesus, did You not say that
he who loves You will be loved of your Father
and that You will love him and manifest Yourself to him? (John 14,21)
Yes, dear Lord, Three in One, strengthen my faith.
"The Kingdom of God is within you" (Luke 17,21).
May I never forget that every time I acquire another degree of grace,
your visit, O Holy Trinity, is renewed.
O Jesus I ponder now your loving words.
"If anyone love me . . . . We will come to him
and make our abode with him" (John 14,23).
Your promise is never exhausted.
It is always living, always new.
But, Lord, my generosity in loving is your gift.
Spur me on always.
Never permit me to rest.
Never allow me to put an obstacle
in the way of your love and your grace.
What an endless horizon I see before me.
After your last supper, You, dear Jesus, told us
that our life of union with the Holy Trinity
is modelled on the union which exists between your own
 Three Persons.
"As You, Father, in Me and I in You;
that they also may be one in us" (John 17,21).
Lord, never cease to diffuse Yourself within my soul.
Father, Son and Holy Spirit, unite me to Yourselves
until I am made perfect in one (John 17,23).
May I ever hasten by faith and love
towards that wonderful goal
which will be my happiness for all eternity.

15 HOLINESS

My holiness is your will, loving Father,
I believe that You will give me all the graces I need.
I confess that without your help I am powerless.
I cannot take one step forward to sanctity.
When I ponder the command of Jesus,
"Be perfect as your heavenly Father is perfect" (Matt. 5,48),
I am filled with a kind of fear.
How is that possible, dear Lord? I ask.
How can I be as perfect as You, heavenly Father,
Who are infinite in all your attributes?
I can only obey such a command by being holy to the fullness of
  my capacity.
Lord, You call all your children to be holy.
Yes, and holy as You are holy.
But each of us is given by You a different capacity.
Fill me with your love according to the capacity You have given me.
I pray that nothing outside You, O loving Father,
will take me from the road to holiness.
I wish to be absorbed wholly by my will to be like You.
I believe that You want me to be holy
infinitely more than I can desire it myself.
I beg You to bring your infinite power to work in me.
Give me faith as strong and undoubting as can be.
Give me hope, confidence and trust that never wavers.
Give me love in all its fullness.
I believe that your divine Son merited all the graces I need.
He is the one source of true holiness.
Lord Jesus, teach me how to learn from your example and
  your teaching.
Then give me the means to live up to all I learn.
I long to imitate You, my dear Jesus.
I know You displayed every virtue in its fullest perfection.
At its best my life can be only a faint reflection of yours.
But I beg You give me the graces I need to be like You.
Do not be content, Lord, with merely offering them to me.
Move my will, my whole being, to use all that You offer.
I know that to be holy I must do all that is my duty
always and exactly,
using my daily life to increase my capacity for perfection.
What a great mystery I discover here, dear Lord.

How often I think about it, dear God!
How truly I know it in my heart!
Holiness does not consist in words and signs
but in loving and doing your will.
My pride is an obstacle in my way.
Transform it, Lord, into true humility.
Force me to be one of your really little lovers,
never forgetting my weakness,
yet daring to trust You perfectly.
Yes, Lord, I know that You offer me all the graces I need
to be the kind of person You want me to be.
Do more, Lord.
Compel me as You alone know how
to accept and use all the helps You offer me.
Make me cling fast to your helps at every moment of every day.
I know I must grow in virtue
but I know that to do this I depend on You.
I try to be an apostle, to lead others to love You,
but I cannot do this unless I love You
and am seen to love You.
Let me never tire in the struggle to be like You.
May my desire for perfection always grow.
Give me the grace to renounce all which keeps me from You.
Take away my blindness so that I shall see clearly
what I ought to seek and what I ought to avoid.
The world and its attractions force themselves on me.
I want to see everything in the light of eternity.
Guide me, dear Lord, in the pleasure I may enjoy.
Enlighten my mind to see everything as You see it.
With every year that passes the consumer society around me
offers more distractions,
more temptations to involvement in luxuries.
May I be wise in my choice
and use nothing in such a way as to keep me from You.
My wish is never to love anything so much
as to make me love You less.
Jesus, may I keep the sight of You ever before me
to inspire me to grow in likeness to You,
first of all in my spiritual life
and then in everything that those around me see in me.

17   I FACE UP TO FAITH

My God, you know me through and through.
In your presence I examine my attitude to belief.
Faith is your gift!
I must base my whole life on it
and every detail of my life.
Heavenly Father, You know how full I am of myself
and of all that is natural.
Help me to get rid of it all, to empty myself of the natural
and to fill the emptiness with all that is supernatural.
I restate my belief (Lord make it vivid).
I am nothing without You.
I have nothing without You.
I can do nothing without You.
Yes, Lord, burn the conviction deep into my soul
Brand me with it.
Without You I am nothing, have nothing and can do nothing.
God, because You love me
You became man.
Jesus, teach me what faith in You really means.
I cannot be in love with You unless I believe in You.
The fervour of my love depends on the reality of my faith.
Teach me, dear Jesus, how to comprehend what your infinite
love means.
Your love is greater than the sum total of all human love.
It is infinitely greater than all the love of all the Saints,
even when I add the love of the angels
and the immense love of your Blessed Mother.
Your love infinitely surpasses all.
You, Jesus, are love.
You were always God therefore always love
throughout a timeless, measureless eternity.
I want to bring home to myself, dear Lord,
what your infinite love really means.
You were infinite love before you were born,
infinite love as a baby in your Mother's arms,
infinite love as a toddler, a teenager, an apprentice.
Infinite love dictated what You said and what You did not say.
Lord, Holy Spirit, brand me I beg with this truth.
Make me grasp it with my whole being.
I wish to love it.

My dear Jesus, help me realise the perfections of your divinity.
In You lies the real mystery of the Church.
Help me understand the full truth about the nature of your Church
as your mystical Body.
Inspire and guide people everywhere to believe
that when they hear the Church they hear You.
Deepen our conviction that when the Church prays You pray,
that the sacrifice of the Church is your sacrifice,
that when a priest forgives, You forgive,
that when the Church unites in marriage You unite.
My dear Lord, move the people of today
to see and reverence You
in the Pope, your Vicar on earth.
Move the members of your mystical Body
to recognize you in the sacraments,
especially in the Holy Eucharist.
Arouse throughout the Church more vital understanding
that Baptism is a new path to divine life,
that Confirmation is a wonderful new visitation of your Holy Spirit,
that the Sacrament of Reconciliation is really your forgiveness,
that Holy Order is your conferring of heavenly powers,
that the Anointing of the Sick is your comforting.
O arouse throughout the world a true understanding
of the uniqueness and inspiration of the Holy Word.
Yes, Lord, may I see You and serve You
in all the folk I meet,
which means that I must regard them as superior to myself.
Grant, Lord, that I may accept the challenge
that radiating You is radiating infinite love.
Brand this with the fire of your Sacred Heart
into the core of my will.
Around me I hear multitudes of voices crying in the wilderness.
You are offering a message of infinite love
to those who do not understand what natural love is.
If only they could be made hungry for the riches of your Church!
I hunger to fill a world that is empty without You.
Lord Jesus, transform me by the gift of faith
to realise the full meaning of surrender to your infinite love.
Help me to fight against superficiality and mediocrity in myself.
May the day soon come when I shall truly be able to say
"I live, not not I, but Christ lives in me" (Gal. 2,20).

19   INTO THE BRIGHT DARKNESS

O God, I know your goodness is infinite.
No finite mind can fathom it.
So in your revelation You have resolved, so to speak,
the white, burning uniform light of your Godhead
into the multiple colour-harmony of your infinite attributes.
Lord, allow me to contemplate those attributes of yours.
Your essence and your attributes are one and the same thing.
I believe that like a very subtle radiance
the splendour of your being three-in-one
is reflected in the order of your attributes.
In the unity of your nature,
You, Father, Son and Holy Spirit, compensate one another.
Into the motionless activity of your sheer being
You convey the august characteristics of your trinity.
You have revealed through the words of St. Peter (2 Peter 1,4)
that my way into your interior is
a participation in your divine nature ever more deeply realized.
When my soul enters into the sublime bright-darkness
of your one divine substance
there takes place its gratuitous affirmation to You, O God.
O wonder of wonders, your divine riches are unfolded in my soul
through your assimilating grace.
I do not merely receive in general a supernatural being and life.
I become, in as far as that is possible
a mirror and reflection of your divine attributes.
Your very limitless perfections tend to pour themselves out, as it were,
over my soul and to imprint on it
the features of your very own countenance.
Yes, O God, I hail You as the bright darkness
for You are infinitely above all conceptional understanding.
I know that if I soar to You as I indeed wish
I must leave all else behind.
To reach You in your infinite simplicity
all thinking and willing, all seeking and yearning are powerless.
I confess, O God, my conviction that You are incomprehensible.
You cannot be confined in a concept.
You are unthinkably beyond all composition.
My words are too heavy to express the nobility of your essence,
too encumbered to be strictly applicable to You.
O that I may love enough the inward secret,
the free, dematerialized reality of all your divine words.

20   TRUE VINE

My Lord Jesus, I long to understand more fully
the wonderful mystery of those who are baptised
becoming one with You.
On the night before your Passion, You said to your apostles,
"I am the true vine; and my Father is the husbandman .   .   .   .
Abide in me, and I in you.
As the branch cannot bear fruit of itself,
unless it abides in the vine,
so neither can you unless you abide in Me." (John 15, 1-4)
Yes, Lord, I do believe
that except through your mediation
I cannot receive the least degree of grace.
A branch detached from the tree
cannot receive even the smallest drop of sap.
You tell me, dear Lord, that when I abide in You
I not only have supernatural life
but I receive special attention from my heavenly Father
the husbandman.
Lord, give me the help I need just to comprehend adequately
what it means to be an adopted child of your Father.
How can I appreciate the full meaning of his love?
How can I even hope to understand the mystery
of his seeing You, dear Jesus, in me?
Fire me with the conviction
and never let me forget it for a moment
that I form, as it were, a living part of You
as a branch forms a living part of the vine.
Yes, when I was baptised I was grafted on to You.
This was only made possible because on the Cross
You died for me.
The cost of this spiritual grafting
was nothing less than your own Precious Blood.
Yes, Lord, by my baptism I am in You.
But You ask far more.
You tell me to abide, to dwell, in You.
I long to become grafted ever more firmly into You.
Only with your grace can I live in union with You,
make You the centre, the heart, the sun of my interior life.
By taking me to abide in You,
You teach me to use all my strength, my mind, my heart, my will
to live in You and by You.

21   JESUS MY ALL

Jesus my Lord, my God, my all.
I really love to say with truth and sincerity
You are everything to me.
My dearest wish is to belong entirely to You.
I want to live only to love You and to serve You.
For me You came into this world.
For me You chose to suffer immense trials.
For me You were mocked and scourged.
For me You remain in the most Blessed Sacrament.
For me You continue the sacrifice of Yourself in Holy Mass.
You feed my soul in Holy Communion.
You are indeed the only way to follow.
You give me your Church, your mystical Body,
to guide and direct me along that way.
Yes Lord, I believe that You are the door
through which I must pass if I wish You
to reveal to me the secret of how to love.
Without You, dear Lord, I am a wanderer.
I am worse, I am nothing.
I long to love You wholly, entirely, in truth
and to have You always at my side.
What more do I need if I have You?
You have given yourself to me and for me.
I am not worthy to be called your friend.
But that is what you said.
"Greater love than this no man has
than that he lay down his life for his friends" (John 15,13).
Yes, dear Lord, You are my dearest friend.
Be my nearest too.
I wish to walk hand in hand with You, the way,
through this valley of tears
a pilgrim preparing for eternity.
Help me to forget myself to walk with You.
I wish to have no will but yours.
Remind me at every moment of your presence.
Teach me how to think and speak and act.
Give me a love of prayer.
Transform my weakness into your strength.
May I grow daily in love of You, my dearest Friend.

My God, every time I turn to You in prayer
I am overcome by the certainty that You can never be fully known.
The very effort to imagine your divine perfections
makes me speechless with wonder and admiration.
I know that whatever thoughts come into my mind
concerning your infinite immensity and greatness
are as nothing in comparison with what remains to be known.
If all the knowledge of all the myriads of angels is put together
it is finite, limited, created.
You are infinite, unlimited, uncreated.
What am I when compared with those angels!
I contemplate as well as I can
the perfections and the beauty of heaven and earth
and all the wonderful creatures in them.
Then I turn to You, my God.
How much more beautiful, more perfect are You, the Creator,
for in You all are contained in a manner infinitely eminent.
Still, dear God, I have to confess the unworthiness of my concepts.
How lowly, how finite they are.
You, mighty God, are not wise or powerful, beautiful or great
in the way my poor mind conceives these perfections.
I confess that You are all these things.
Yes, indeed, but in a way so different which my created intellect
 cannot comprehend.
Your grandeur, all your perfections, every attribute
all are infinite, immense, ineffable, incomprehensible.
All are in You, O God, being, power, activity.
Through the grandeur of your works
I know the greatness of the power from which they proceed.
Through the immensity of this power
I know the excellence of your Being.
Lord, I beg to be able to leave behind all the creatures of heaven
and earth,
to soar far beyond all that can be sensed, imagined or
humanly understood, to arrive at last at your substance
which surpasses all sensation and understanding
which infinitely surpasses all that is created.
O God, You are the one light beyond all light,
the one beauty exceeding all beauty,
the one substance above all substance,
the one life surpassing all life.

23   GOD, INFINITE LOVE

"God is charity" Holy Writ tells me of You, dear Lord.
Not, "in God there is charity" or merely
"God is infinitely loving"
but "God is love" (1 John 4,16)
Everything in you, O God, is love.
Lord, strengthen my understanding of what it means.
You are essentially love.
In You love is an infinite will for good.
It is directed towards infinite good,
your very being, your essence in which you delight.
Your love, O God, I believe is an infinite
complacent love of your own infinite goodness.
By an act of love You brought creatures into existence.
You created them, You love them for your own glory.
You call us to share in the sublime life of love
which is your very self.
For this purpose You pour grace into my soul.
Yes, Lord, help me to understand in faith
how charity, love, is your Being,
your essence, your life.
You are all love.
Everything in You is love.
You are that sovereign love
by which You love yourself from all eternity.
You take infinite pleasure in your limitless Being
In love you beget your infinite, timeless, eternal Word.
You love the Word, the figure of your substance.
O infinite Word, You love the Father from whom You proceed.
Enlighten me, verify my faith, to understand how
the charity by which You, O God, love Yourself
is so infinitely perfect that it constitutes a Person,
the Holy Spirit, the third Person of the most holy Trinity.
Surely here is enough contemplation for more than a lifetime.
Give me a vivid insight, heavenly Father, into the love You have
in knowing your Son and your Son in knowing You
and into the ardour with which the Holy Spirit unites with You.
Why do so few people trouble to contemplate
your infinite, eternal love, the love by which You,
Father, Son and Holy Spirit know each other,
love each other, and delight in each other?
Lord, enlighten my faith that I may effectively understand.

24 LOVING

When I consider that You, O God, are love
and how your love has been poured out
on all You have made
I find it strange that You have to command men to love You.
Your command must be an act of your love
for You cannot act apart from what You are
and You are love.
How indebted I am to You, O God,
for the happiness and honour of being able to love You.
I can never thank You enough for the privilege.
Still more, I can never hope to thank You
for commanding me to love You.
Lord, when I contemplate all your infinite attributes
I feel forced to love them all.
They are your very self.
When I love your love, I love your beauty,
your wisdom, your knowledge, your power, your mercy.
Faith is your gift.
Strengthen my faith daily so that
my love will grow ever more incisive.
Dear eternal Father, I think of heaven.
I look forward to being utterly ravished
by the vision of your infinite attributes.
Here my love is weakened by my earthiness,
by passions, temptations, the materialism around me.
In heaven I shall be wholly free of passions.
There will be nothing to distract me.
No anxieties will trouble my mind.
Nothing will thwart my powers.
O what a thought—perpetual, uninterrupted love!
May I begin to experience it even now!
May I never deliberately fall short of trying to love You
with all my heart, with all my soul,
with all my mind, with all my strength.
O yes, dear Lord, I know that without You
I cannot take even a step forward to my salvation.
This thought inspires me to pray even more fervently to You.
You could not have commanded me to love You so completely
unless You were offering me the grace so to do.
O dear Lord, convince me of the loveableness of your love.

25 THE HOLY SPIRIT

Holy Spirit of God, come to me.
Make me realise that You, infinite God,
are living within me.
I recall the words You inspired Paul to write: "God sent the Spirit of his
Son into our hearts crying Abba, Father" (Gal. 4,6). Teach me the way
of spiritual childhood. Permit me to contemplate the infinite
perfections of God just so that I may comprehend the immensity of his
love in bidding me to pray to Him as a Father.
I believe that I must try to live as a member of the divine family,
not as a servant but as a friend,
and more than a friend, a child.
With the grace You have given me
I share your divine nature.
I can know and love in the way You, O God,
have known and love Yourself for a timeless eternity.
You invest me with sonship.
You impregnate me with the dispositions of a son.
You must wish my life to be just one long cry of "Abba, Father".
O yes, dear Lord, I believe that alone, by itself,
with only its own resources
no created nature can look upon You.
I thank You for giving me the wonder of supernatural life,
a created miniature of your very own divine nature,
which raises me up, makes me capable
of seeing You, face to face, unveiled.
Holy Spirit, You inspired the Apostle to tell us
that grace is diffused in our hearts by You.
It comes directly from your presence.
Pour your gift of understanding into me, O divine Spirit,
so that I can appreciate the wonder of the divine quality
which so transforms and dignifies my soul.
By it I am born again, made holy.
Within me now shines the sun of a better, a higher world,
the divine light of true life.
Holy Spirit, be with me always.
Be to me what Jesus was to his Apostles.
May I always remember your presence in my soul
as my teacher, my consoler, my advocate, my counsellor,
my intercessor, my defender, my best friend.

26 ANOTHER PARACLETE

Holy Spirit, Spirit of Truth,
teach me to know You and to love You.
Jesus told his Apostles that He would send *another* Paraclete.
He had been the Paraclete.
You, I believe, were to be to the disciples
what Jesus was before He left them.
I bring the picture before my mind.
I hear Jesus teaching the Twelve to believe, to pray and to endure,
filling them with courage to convert the world,
inspiring them with noble ambitions,
comforting them in their inadequacy,
receiving them back to his love when they repented,
acting as father and mother to them,
being in fact their all.
For Him they had left all else— parents, relatives, friends, home,
occupations, wealth, freedom. How shocked they were when Jesus
told them He would leave them.
But You, divine Spirit, were to take his place.
He told them that You would abide with them forever.
Holy Spirit, pour your graces into the minds and hearts of
people to-day
so that all will believe fervently, that, just as Jesus did when He lived,
walked, talked and ate with his Apostles,
You teach the Church,
ever prompting, inspiring and consoling.
You are with your Church, living in each soul,
by your seven gifts bringing us into communication with You.
These gifts are the fullness of Christ of which we all receive.
Holy Spirit help me to understand
how You anoint us,
how You take up your abode within us,
how You dwell in us as in a Temple,
how You rest on us as You rested on Jesus,
how You are given to us as sign, character, pledge and consecration,
how we partake of You, are held and possessed by You,
how we live and work and are led, loved and driven by You.
Holy Spirit, I thank You for enabling your Church
to receive what could not be received by nature.
Spirit of God, You are the flame which must not be extinguished.

27   LIVING IN THE SPIRIT

Holy divine Spirit, You inspired Paul to say
that if we live by You we must walk by You (Gal. 5,25).
May it always be clear that I try to live by You.
May I never be guided by purely human judgements and wisdom.
May the conviction deepen and grow in me
that I must live as a citizen of God's kingdom.
Inspire me, lead me, divine Spirit,
to adopt your sense of values, the rules of the supernatural.
From the bottom of my heart I long for supernatural understanding,
for enlightenment, for the gift of being right,
for a firm, luminous grasp of conclusions
to love and enjoy what is right from God's angle.
Give me that holy fear which You describe
as the beginning of wisdom (Prov. 1,7).
Fill me with habitual attention and reverence for God.
Enable me to live always in sight of my last end,
evaluating everything from the standpoint of eternity.
I wish consciously to belong to God.
You know, divine Spirit, how I dread to lose God,
how fearful I am of acting according to mere human reason,
the promptings of sense, emotion or worldly prudence.
The ways of the world are not your ways.
Bring love to me.
Form me in true divine love.
Give me a tender, affectionate, childlike disposition
to You, the Father and the Son.
In reparation for all those around me who neglect You
I choose You, loving Spirit, here and now,
just as those of the world choose their friends,
to be my supreme interest.
I long to love You, to care for You,
to make You, O God, the main object of my knowledge.
Yes, eternal Trinity, Father, Son and Holy Spirit,
I want to think about You more than I think about anything else.
I want to be obsessed by the thought of You,
to be magnetised by You,
to contemplate You in all your fullness,
to rouse my whole being to praise You,
to surrender myself completely to You.

Divine Spirit of Love, You know me through and through.
You know how fervently I long
to make the interests of God my main concern.
I have no deeper conviction
than that God loves me.
May I be engrossed by the earthly life of the infinite God
in his Church,
in the blessed Eucharist,
in souls.
May I love as fervently as You will me to
the Mother of Jesus who was always
so closely and indissolubly united with Him.
Holy Spirit, purify my gaze so that
every trace of God on earth will be precious to me.
May I grow in love of your Saints
because You, God, love them
and they return and reflect your love.
Holy Spirit, I believe that surrender to You
means conflict with the devil and the flesh
and especially with the world.
But You teach me that the life of love
never loses a peace that is deep, substantial and fundamental.
Holy Spirit, teach me the spirit of obedience.
Strengthen me to fulfil the duties of my state of life,
doing what I ought to do,
when I ought to do it,
and as I ought to do it.
Keep me balanced.
Guide me to suspect whatever is extraordinary or unusual.
Inspire me to use rightly my tongue.
Teach me charity, moderation, faith, control.
May I use human affection to make me love You more.
Spirit of Love, may I always adore
the eternal Trinity living in my soul.
Increase my spirit of surrender.
You know infinitely better than I do
my many weaknesses, the poverty of my spirit, my helplessness.
I thank You now for all You have done for me,
for your presence in my soul,
for your graces, helps, inspirations, virtues, gifts
and the fruits of them.

29   PERSEVERANCE

Heavenly Father, I pray as your child.
Help me never to be discouraged.
I often fail; I am troubled by doubts;
I am criticised; I am even attacked and misjudged.
I am all too human.
You know how sincere I am in longing for holiness,
to give myself to You, to abandon myself to your will,
to work for the salvation of souls.
Give me more confidence in your presence with me.
I know, loving Father, that You desire my holiness
infinitely more than I desire it myself.
Give me courage to keep on keeping on when things are hard,
when everything seems to be against me,
when I am unable to find sympathetic advisers,
when the future seems black,
when what I conscientiously believe to be wrong
seems to be gaining ground.
Lord, give me courage then
to swim against the stream rather than with it.
Move me to think of eternity, the end of my life,
to ask myself now what then I would wish to have done.
Give me patience, Lord.
Cure me of my habit of expecting too much too soon.
Give me the grace to live according to the advice I give others.
Never let me forget that Good Friday
is always followed by Easter Sunday.
Give me the conviction that no road is too long
when I advance along it deliberately, step by step, without
   undue haste.
Strengthen my belief that nothing is as important
as a growing in love for You,
no cause so worthwhile as work for You.
Give me power to concentrate on what is most important.
Lord Jesus, You tell me to abide in You
and You promise to abide in me.
Alone I am powerless to do even this.
Take hold of me; place me in the very midst of your love.
Lord, You kept keeping on on the road to Calvary.
From your childhood You were surrounded by deadliest enemies.
But You persevered until they crucified You.
Teach me, dearest Lord, to keep walking on the narrow way to heaven.

Dearest Jesus, help me to pray about your life.
You were only a baby when Herod tried to murder You.
When You remained in the Temple
even your Mother seemed to rebuke You.
In your public life they put the worst interpretations on your actions.
You ate with people and they called You a glutton.
You taught with loving wisdom and understanding
but your words were warped, twisted, falsely reported,
made to mean the opposite, turned into half-truths against You.
The representatives of your Father, the priests,
should have supported You.
They did just the opposite.
With people, too, You failed.
Some walked no more with You.
Of some You said their hearts were far from You.
When You offered them Yourself in the blessed Eucharist
they refused to believe You.
O Jesus, I try to enter your mind as You hear them say
"Can anything good come out of Nazareth?" (John 1,46).
"You have a devil" (John 7,20).
"He seduces the people" (John 7,12).
You worked miracles but they remained unconvinced.
Those You cured failed to thank You.
Because You were too good
they laughed You to scorn.
You allowed Yourself to be tempted by Satan.
Your friends deserted You.
Your chosen one betrayed You.
Your strong one denied You.
Those You had helped cried out "Not this man but Barabbas"
(John 18,40).
They struck, mocked, flogged and crucified You.
Lord, why should I expect my efforts at good
to be appreciated?
Lord, help me to persevere in the hard way.
Mary, Mother of Perseverance,
Virgin most faithful, pray for me.
Your perseverance brought you to the foot of the Cross.
Your reward was to be assumed into heaven.

31 THE POWER OF GOD

"Nothing is impossible to God" (Luke 1, 37).
So said the announcing Gabriel.
O God, how did You manifest your infinite power?
You created heaven and earth.
I cannot begin to understand what even this means.
Earthly minds are baffled by the sun, the moon and the stars.
Day after day more is discovered about them.
Your revealed word tells of myriads of celestial spirits.
You created this beautiful world and all things in it.
All human thought, all the discoveries of science,
all the true conclusions of the philosophers,
all the achievements of our race since You created it—
all came from You.
So do all the wonders of nature.
Even the simplest flower is beyond man's power to create.
I believe, O God, that You not only created all things
but You govern and sustain them.
"My Father works until now, and I work" said your divine Son
(John 5,17).
No creature perishes nor is deprived of anything
How pregnant with meaning are the simple words of Jesus,
"Are not two sparrows sold for a farthing?
And not one of them should fall to the ground without your Father.
But the very hairs of your head are all numbered.
Fear not, therefore;
better are you than many sparrows" (Matt. 10, 28-31).
Who can fathom or ever hope to understand such power?
Yes, dear Lord, as I ponder how You created and govern all things
I just begin to realise something of your omnipotence.
Your goodness in making out of nothing
everything that exists outside Yourself
is the effect of your infinite love,
of your limitless wisdom in directing and sustaining all in
perfect harmony,
of your indescribable liberality in doing all this for the benefit
of mankind and of your unfathomable mercy.
Time after time we have offended You
but You have never destroyed creation.

My dear God, when can I hope to understand your love?
You know how often I recall that You created me,
that I owe everything I am to You.
I know that I ought to love You in return.
But so should all the human beings You created.
They should return your creative love.
But they do not.
Therefore You came down from heaven
to win the love of your creatures.
All You have done for them adds up to an almost endless litany.
The culmination of your love was your Passion and Death.
You were crucified to move men to love You.
You did so much more.
You gave us your Church and the Sacraments.
Through them we can share in your own divine nature.
You gave us above all the Blessed Sacrament.
How can I express in words
the love contained in that gift?
Your Holy Spirit inspired your beloved disciple
to put it so very simply,
"God is love", he said (1 John 4,8).
Yes, O infinite God, You loved me
long before I was capable of returning your love.
I recall other inspired words through your Prophet,
"I have loved you with an everlasting love,
therefore have I drawn you, taking pity on you" (Jer. 31,3).
O my God, I repeat my acts of faith.
Out of love You created me.
Out of love You saved me through your Son.
Out of love You adopted me as your child.
Out of love You sanctified me through the Holy Spirit.
Out of love You warn me.
Out of love You punish me.
Out of love You forgive me.
O my God, brand the truth on my very soul:
You are not only loving, You are love itself.
With my whole mind and heart and soul and being
I believe that You love me.
Let me not forget that your love for me
calls for my love in return.

33 A TREASURE OF LOVE

"Our Father who art in heaven."
Yes, O God, infinite Being, limitless perfection,
You permit me to call You Father.
The title implies love.
You love me not just as one of your creatures
but as your very own special child.
You want me to love You as my Father.
I try to think of human fatherhood,
of all the tales and romances concerned with it
but the sum total of all human fatherly love
is less than a faint shadow of You, my heavenly Father.
How can I ever express in words what I feel for You.
You are a treasure of love, of beauty, of goodness, of comfort
beyond words.
O my loving Father, give me in your love
the gift to understand your love
to make the thought of it affect everything in my life.
May your fatherly love brighten my loneliness.
May it make me see every pain and sorrow in a different light.
May it give me courage when I feel so utterly powerless.
May it make me turn to You to solve the mysteries
I cannot hope to understand alone.
Dear Father, take my mind into your loving care.
Make my knowledge, remembrance
and deep understanding of all You are
my guiding light through the darkness of my earthly pilgrimage.
I believe that in your fatherly love You are always shielding me,
protecting me from evils and dangers I never even notice.
I beg You, Father dear, to cause me to remember
that the effects of your fatherhood are ever with me.
Your blessings are like the stars in the heavens.
They are far too many for me even to begin to know.
I think of them—my being, my knowledge, my sight,
my hearing, my health, my speech, my family,
my friends, my faith, my church, my sacraments—
yes, Lord, the list is endless.
But they are all components of your loving Fatherhood.
Bless me at every moment, in every place.
Bless those I love and those I ought to love.
Forgive me for having failed to live as your child.

34 GOOD SHEPHERD

My dear Jesus, You called Yourself the Good Shepherd.
In your immense love You care for every member of your flock.
Like the shepherds You knew on earth
You always wish to go before, to lead your flock.
Help me to lead others to You.
Inspire me to display qualities which will lead others to trust me.
Breathe into me the spirit of friendliness, gentleness, understanding,
sympathy, loyalty, genuine affection, approachableness,
all combined with firmness.
Lord, keep me balanced.
Give me the common sense that is true wisdom.
Lord, I pray for those I see around me
falling for everything that is new.
Help me to help others by showing myself to be
neither too progressive nor too conservative.
"I know mine and mine know me", You said (John 10,14).
O Lord, I long to respond by the dedication of my life
to your personal devotion to me.
I long to repay your love by my love,
your devotedness by my devotedness,
your sacrifice by my reparation.
You gave yourself for me;
I wish to give myself to You
with a love that is true, deep, personal and sacrificial.
Your words, dear Jesus, take me to the heart of the Trinity,
"I know mine and mine know me;
as the Father knows me and I know the Father" (John 10,15).
Your love and your Father's love are infinite.
My love can never be that,
but it can exhaust my capacity.
I long to love You with the greatest love possible.
Lord, grant that I may see all in the love of your Heart.
"I lay down my life for my sheep," You said (John 10,15).
How can I thank You enough for that?
How can I ever hope to comprehend
what the Prince of your Apostles wrote,
saying that we have been redeemed by your Precious Blood
as of an unblemished and spotless lamb (1 Peter 1,19).
Lord, I wish my life to be saturated by love,
bound up with the idea of sacrifice, always united with You.

35   MAY I ALWAYS LOVE

My God, may I love You always
for Yourself alone
and not for my consolation.
I want to obey your command
to love You with my whole heart.
I shall not be satisfied, dear Lord,
until all my powers are engaged in loving You.
I believe that the substance of my act of love
is not in my feelings but in my will.
Give me grace, therefore, not to depend on my emotions.
I wish to rise above them,
to love when I feel neither warmth nor consolation.
I believe, dear Lord, that You may take consolations away from me
to make my love more pure, more mature, more meritorious.
May I always will with determination
just what You will.
May I always desire your good pleasure and delight
above all else.
O God, I long to wish good to You
at every moment of every day
You permit me to live.
I sincerely wish to use all my strength
in living for You, to please You.
I offer You now all the dryness I feel in prayer.
I wish to set on You alone
my feelings, my joy, my contentment, my love.
Convince me by your grace
that true love and union with You
consist in the pure operation of my will,
seeking You and your will above everything.
May I hunger and thirst for You alone.
May my love of your will,
my complete abandonment to your love
take me completely out of myself.
May my whole life be enclosed in your will.
O Jesus, divine Master, You proved your love
by being crucified for me.
May I walk along the way of love
with no thought of self-interest
living only for You and union with your divine loving will.

36 LOURDES

Heavenly Father, I thank You for Lourdes
and all it has meant to your Church and the world.
May the whole world come to realise the significance of it all.
The Vicar of Christ, your only begotten Son,
invoked his infallibility to proclaim that the Blessed Virgin Mary
was conceived free from any stain of sin.
Then, in your loving kindness, You willed
that she herself should appear to Bernadette
and proclaim that she was indeed the Immaculate Conception.
I thank You, good Lord, for thus approving
not only the truth the Pope had defined
but also his use of his prerogative of infallibility in defining it.
Lord, cause all who would follow You to see in this
a proof of the truth of your Church.
Yes, Lord, I believe that the Pope is preserved from error
because he is the visible head of your one Church.
Then, good Lord, You willed that all this should be verified
through the miracles that have taken place.
"If you believe not my words" Jesus once said,
"Then look at my works. These give testimony of Me" (John 10,38).
So it is at Lourdes.
But dear Lord, there is much more to be understood.
I beg You, enlighten the minds of your children
to understand that the Blessed Virgin was conceived immaculate
because she was the mother of God.
I believe that Lourdes is a wonderful mirror
in which those who have eyes to see
behold implicitly the evidence that the Pope is infallible
because he is the visible head of the one Church of Christ
and that Mary is immaculate
because she is the mother of God.
But there is more, dear Lord.
Lourdes soon became a shrine of the Blessed Sacrament
Mary led those who venerated her
to the eucharistic presence of your Son and hers.
So, Lord, God loving Father,
I thank You with all my heart
for all that Lourdes signifies for the true believer
and I beg You, illumine more minds with this truth.

37   TO JESUS

My Jesus, strengthen my belief that You are God the Son.
Loving Son of Mary, make me love her as You did.
Jesus, You are the Truth. Never cease to instruct me.
Jesus, You are the Way. Always direct me.
Jesus, You are the Life. May I always live in and for you.
Jesus, You are the Prince of Peace. Let nothing disturb my peace of soul.
Jesus, You are the eternal High Priest. May I never cease to offer sacrifice with You. Jesus, You are a model of patience.
Jesus, meek and humble of heart. Make my heart like yours.
Jesus, my Redeemer. Save me from sin.
Jesus, my Lord and my God. Make and keep me always yours.
Jesus, the one Mediator. Reconcile me to your Father.
Jesus, physician of my soul, strengthen and heal me.
Jesus, my final Judge. Ever absolve me.
Jesus, my King, govern me with your wisdom.
Jesus, all holy, sanctify me.
Jesus, abyss of goodness, make and keep me always truly good.
Jesus, living bread from heaven, feed the life of my soul.
Jesus, Father of the prodigal, receive me into your loving embrace.
Jesus, joy of my soul, enliven my spiritual life.
Jesus, my keeper, sustain me in virtue.
Jesus, magnet of love, draw me more closely to You.
Jesus, my protector, shield me against temptation.
Jesus, my hope, sustain and support me.
Jesus, object of my love, make me love You as I should.
Jesus, fountain of life, purify me.
Jesus, infinite power, strengthen my longing for holiness.
Jesus, example of patience, teach me how to cope with frustration.
Jesus, exalted for your obedience, show me how to see God's will everywhere.
Jesus, lover of chastity, give me grace to subdue my flesh.
Jesus, zealous for souls, pour the grace of zeal into my sluggish will.
Jesus, lover of poverty, detach me from all but You.
Jesus, Good Shepherd, feed, protect and guide me as your sheep.
Jesus, divine teacher, guide me by your infinite wisdom.
Jesus, infinite goodness, fill me with real love, kindness and mercy.
Jesus, abyss of all virtues, implant every virtue into my heart.
Jesus, infinite Victim, may I give all that I am and have to You.

38   SURRENDER TO GOD'S WILL

Lord, I believe most firmly
that your divine will must be the rule of my life,
the direct and safe way.
Guide me to embrace it and to follow it bravely and faithfully.
Grant me this grace, loving Father,
to entrust myself entirely to You.
Preserve my soul in peace
free from worries which have nothing to do with my duty now.
Sustain me, Lord, in all my efforts to abandon myself to your will.
May I recognise your artifices in all that affects me.
May I fervently believe that my present trials
will one day be a source of great joy.
May I understand that the more I seem to lose
by giving to You, the more I gain.
Help me to realise and understand more firmly than I do now
that the most ordinary things are channels of grace,
but that the grace is often concealed.
Help me, too, to remember that by seeking and loving your holy will
I need never worry about those who work against me.
When my ideas, my lights, my reasonings, my plans and ambitions
are rejected or unrealised
help me to see your will, your love at work.
Lord I do believe that your will is the expression of infinite love,
goodness, wisdom, justice and power.
It is the source of all good.
Strengthen my conviction that the way to peace
is the way of loving abandonment to your will.
This is what the angels promised to the shepherds
as they announced the birth of your Son.
I long, Lord, to be an effective instrument in your hands.
I know that I can be this only if I love your holy will.
I try to belong to You entirely,   ·
to accept and love your will in every detail at every moment.
I leave all my past to your infinite mercy.
I entrust the future to your loving Providence.
I wish to act at every present moment in perfect surrender to your will.
Dear Lord Jesus, may I learn through abandonment to your will
to love by You, with You and in You.
May I always love and do, Lord, what You will.

39   THE FIRST STATION

Jesus, You are the sinless judge of all men,
all knowing, all true, all loving, all just.
Your creatures condemned You
for no reason and without a fair trial.
The people amongst whom You had lived,
to whom You had given your teaching of infinite wisdom,
for whom You had worked marvellous miracles
shouted for your crucifixion and death.
The High Priests, representatives of your eternal Father,
Pontius Pilate, a poor pagan weakling,
knew that You were innocent but condemned You.
Oh, how different would have been their actions
if they had known that at the end of time
You will come on the clouds,
with your mighty angels,
in great power and majesty,
to judge all the world.
They would have fallen on their knees
to adore You with fear and trembling
and to beg for your mercy.
Before your jury, Lord, You were silent.
Now, even more profoundly You conceal your majesty
in the most Blessed sacrament.
Yet by right yours is the same splendour of the glory
that one day will cause the sun to fade and the earth to tremble.
May I never cease to adore You, Lord.
Is there anything You have not done
to save me from eternal damnation?
You said that he who eats You
will live by You
and that he who eats the bread You give
will live forever.
You remain always with me.
You long to come into my soul every day.
You give me Yourself as a pledge of eternal life.
I thank You, dear Lord.
I beg You to give me all the graces I need
to respond as I should to all You have done for me,
especially in the most Holy Eucharist.

O Jesus, from all eternity You saw your cross.
You knew that by it You would save the human race.
You are infinite love.
So when You were bidden carry your cross
You embraced it, kissed it, as the instrument
You would use to prove your love.
It was the will of your eternal Father
that by your agony and death on the cross
sinners would be saved.
Before time was created
You looked forward to this moment.
In the timeless eternity ever present before You
were all the sins of all men.
You saw the sins of the pagans who did not know You.
But You saw also the sins of those to whom You chose
to give the virtue of faith.
The sins of those You had chosen in your Providence
to receive this precious gift
must have required special satisfaction from You—
sins against the Church,
sins against the Pope,
sins against the truth You revealed,
sins against the gifts of your Sacraments,
sins especially against the Sacrament of your love.
The terrible scenes of that Good Friday
when You first embraced your cross
are repeated against your Real Presence in our churches.
You embraced your cross as a supreme act of love.
Dear Jesus, I want so much to make reparation
for all those who to-day deny You
as Peter did to a serving girl,
for all those who betray You
for earthly wealth as Judas did,
for all those who by their lack of devotion
flee away from You as your chosen Apostles did.
Lord, I want you to be at the very centre of my life.
The Holy Eucharist is You.
May a small part of my cross
united with the cross You lovingly embraced
be the little self-denial entailed in loving your Eucharistic presence
as I should.

41 THE THIRD STATION

O what a mystery of faith.
Jesus, I believe that You are God Almighty,
the Second Person of the most adorable trinity,
infinite in every perfection.
Adored by the countless angels You created
but now crushed to the ground beneath a criminal's cross.
You are infinite Wisdom.
The whole universe is in your hands.
The most renowned scientists discover laws your wisdom made.
Now I see You fall.
The creatures whom You chose to make
in preference to all the others you might have made,
cheat you, mock you, kick you.
O infinite humility.
Falling beneath your cross
You atone for all the pride of the world
including my own.
Jesus, You reign now with infinite power.
You reign for every consecrated host,
from every tabernacle in every church,
from every Benediction throne.
You support and govern the world.
By your loving Providence you guide the destinies of men.
As You hid your majesty as You fell under your Cross,
so You hide it even more in the Sacred Host.
You seem so weak, so abject.
You abandon yourself to the caprices of your servants.
Yes, dear Lord, I know of the sacrileges against your Real Presence.
I know of the dreadful neglect of thousands of your children.
I know of the frustrated desires of your Sacred Heart
too often refused entry into the souls of your children.
Most of those who witnessed your fall under the Cross
had never been given by You the gift of faith.
But now, how many millions were made your children in baptism
and received the gift of faith
but now live as if your eucharistic presence never existed!
Yes, Lord, and how many are too proud to believe
that the tiny Host is really and truly your infinite Self.
Lord, I long to be humble enough to believe
and to make reparation for all those who do not believe.

O Mary, my dearest Mother, I stand by you in spirit
as you see your Son carrying his Cross.
You are the Queen of Creation,
the sublimest work of God.
By your free consent God the Son
was able to take from your sinless body
the body you saw carrying his Cross,
the body which was to be nailed to it
and die on it.
Even more than the highest angel
you understood the mystery which was being enacted.
As He drew near to you, you saw Him,
the High Priest for ever, according to the order of Melchisedech.
You saw also the Infinite Victim,
precious enough to redeem a million worlds.
Now I can meet that very same Jesus
almost whenever I wish by visiting him in the Tabernacle.
I can stand beneath his Cross
as his one sacrifice continues in Holy Mass.
Pray that my faith will be adequate enough
to draw every possible grace from the Holy Eucharist.
Obtain for me from the Holy Spirit
his gift of understanding to enable me to penetrate
more and more, deeper and deeper,
the inexhaustible depths of this mystery of love.
You know, better than any other, his yearning
to enter souls in Holy Communion.
You know how He longs to draw all men to Himself
as He continues the one sacrifice of Calvary in Holy Mass.
Pray for the Church, the mystical Body of your Son
that throughout its multitudes of members
a truly deep and fruitful faith in the Blessed Eucharist
will never cease to grow.
Mother dear, pray especially for all those who sinfully miss Mass
and so fail to wait as you did to see Jesus passing by.
Pray that more of your children will visit your Jesus.
Pray that many more will daily receive
Him fervently and lovingly in Holy Communion.

43   THE FIFTH STATION

O Jesus, in spirit I walk with you to Calvary.
I see the crowds of people along the way,
some extremely hostile, some sad, some simply mesmerised.
Your steps become slower and slower.
Your cruel guards talk among themselves.
They wonder who You are and what You have done.
They think You may not make it to Calvary,
so they force a pagan to carry the Cross with You.
O my dear Lord, what a profound mystery is here.
You are God from God, Lord of lords, King of kings,
with countless hosts of angels ready to carry out your every behest.
But now your true greatness is so hidden
that one of your creatures is compelled to help You.
Lord, in your Church You still walk the way of the Cross.
You are surrounded by unbelievers.
Those who notice You still laugh You to scorn.
You are still denied by the modern Peters,
still betrayed by the Judases.
But there are far too few ready to help You.
Many will agree that their faith is their greatest treasure
but so few, so very few, are ready to try to share the gift.
Good Lord, the need today is sad and grave.
You must know it, for You know everything.
Move then, more of your children to become active members of
the Church.
You live in our churches
ever really, truly and substantially present.
You must have suffered in Gethsemane and throughout your Passion
for all those who are indifferent to You.
There are so many who seem to attend Mass
only because the law of the Church forces them to do so.
They are like Simon, compelled to help You.
Lord, how weak, truly weak, is faith in the Blessed Eucharist
I am sad when I see so very few people at daily Mass,
so few regularly visiting You in the tabernacle,
so few at Benediction,
such a minority receiving You frequently in Holy Communion.
By your almighty power You can reverse this sad situation.
I beg You, Lord, to release a torrent of graces
so that tepidity, indifference and selfishness
will be transformed into zeal, love and generosity.

44 THE SIXTH STATION

O my Jesus, if only I could see You face to face!
As day follows day we recognise people by their faces.
With what love your dear Mother and her husband Joseph
gazed on your face when they saw it first at Bethlehem.
The children of Egypt must have seen your beauty as a child.
The boys and girls of Nazareth were privileged to see your
noble countenance.
For all who met You in your village life
your face was the index of your perfect mind.
Allow me, good Lord, to imagine what those of whom
the Gospels speak discerned in your face.
What did those for whom You worked miracles see?
What did those whose sins You forgave see?
What did Peter see as You gazed on him?
What did Judas, Caiphus, Pilate or Herod see?
Yes, and countless others too.
All saw the most compelling beauty of God the Son.
But now your face, Lord, the splendid mirror of divine majesty
is horribly disfigured with bruises, sweat, spittle and blood.
What defilement has man's depravity caused?
I recall the words of the Prophet, "There is no beauty in him,
no comeliness
and we have seen him, and there was no sightliness,
that we should be attracted to him
Despised and the most abject of men,
a man of sorrows and acquainted with infirmity,
and his look was as it were hidden and despised" (Isaiah 53, 2-3).
Give me, Lord, the courage of Veronica.
Give me her love, her sympathy, her compassion,
which tried to remove the defilement caused by man's depravity.
May I mentally see your sacred face in the consecrated host
elevated at Mass or displayed in the monstrance.
Even now we hear of sacrileges against your sacramental presence.
Even now You are unrecognised by the many
as You were on the way to Calvary.
You have appealed for reparation and atonement.
Give me grace to believe even more firmly
in your eucharistic presence.
Then, dear Lord, do to me what You did to Veronica's towel.
Imprint your likeness on my soul.

45   THE SEVENTH STATION

O Jesus, I contemplate You falling again under your Cross.
I hear the shouts of the crowds.
I see how the soldiers treat You so cruelly.
What a mystery is here.
I believe that You are He for whom the nations sighed.
Of You Isaias cried out,
"O that thou wouldst rend the heavens and come down" (Isaiah 54,1).
For You the angels would sing,
"Lift up your gates, O ye princes,
and the King of Glory shall enter in" (Ps. 23,7).
Yes, princes and people should have escorted You to the
Mount of Sion
with shouts of joy, with pomp and splendour.
But now You are cast out of the city with ignominy,
led by a procession of mockery and derision.
Again I think of the words of the Prophet, ever so true,
"He has borne our infirmities and carried our sorrows,
and we have taken him for a leper,
and as one struck by God and afflicted.
But he was wounded for our iniquities and bruised for our sins.
On him fell the punishment that brought us salvation,
and by his wounds we have been healed" (Isaiah 53, 4-5).
Lord, You were brought down by the weight of the Cross.
I am overcome by the desires of my flesh or the attractions of
the world.
You preferred to fall rather than let go of the Cross.
That is how You heal the lack of love that casts me down.
I open my heart to You, dear Lord.
I still long to go forward along the narrow way
but always with more love, more trust, more strength.
I abandon myself wholly to You.
Take my past. Take my present. Take my future.
I offer You all I have to suffer,
the big things, the little things,
the physical pains, the mental and spiritual anguish.
You, Lord, staggered to your feet
to walk on to still greater pain.
Lord, help me to persevere along your way.
Move your people to honour You in your eucharistic tabernacles.
Too many ignore You; too many are tepid towards You.
Fill them with warm faith and ardent love
so that they will come with You to the daily Calvary of Holy Mass.

O Lord Jesus, were these women who met You
remembering happier days spent with You
when everybody cried out in amazement,
"He has done all things well"? (Mark 7,37).
How kind were your words, dear Lord!
How You wished the world to know that your own sufferings
were not the thing most to be lamented.
You wanted all to learn that your Passion would not stop
the terrible catastrophe that was about to befall Jerusalem.
Present to You were the days of horror that lay ahead
when the natural joy that mothers take in their children
would be turned to grief, all the heavier because
they would be unable to rescue them from the universal ruin.
I contemplate the Saints bursting into tears
at the thought of your sufferings, Lord.
Your words now are an appeal for contrition.
Lord, I beg grace to repent of the times I have offended You.
I wish I could make reparation for the inexhaustible malice of sin.
O Lord, why do millions care not at all that You died for them?
These women on the way to Calvary were a tiny group.
They stand out from the thousands of those who did not care.
So it is to-day—your true lovers are so few.
Lord, I know You are always near to me.
You constantly remind me of my duty and my destiny.
May I never fail to accept your lessons, your warnings, your graces.
You wish me to give a supernatural meaning
to everything I do.
That is my will, too, dearest Lord.
In my heart I want to be thinking of You always
but I am so weak, so very feeble, so inconstant.
My desires are so lofty, my accomplishments so lowly.
Especially hidden in the Sacrament of your love, O Lord,
You receive so little of the love that is due to You.
Yes, I know well the terrible sacrileges recorded in history.
But your loving Heart suffered in Gethsemane,
on the way of the Cross and throughout your Passion
for all the tepidity, meanness of devotion, lack of fervour
shown by the multitude, even of believers
towards this infinitely precious gift of Yourself.
Lord, take me. I want to be all yours—for ever.

47 THE NINTH STATION

Dear Lord, this must have been the worst of your falls.
Calvary was so near.
You could no longer stay on your feet.
You lay on the ground utterly exhausted.
The words of Isaiah were being fulfilled.
"He offered Himself up because it was his will;
abused and ill-treated he opened not his mouth,
as a sheep led to the slaughter,
as a lamb before its shearers" (Is. 53,7)
I beg to enter into your Heart, Lord,
to contemplate your anguish at this moment.
Everyone is against You.
The crowds from the city, visitors from abroad.
How the Scribes and Pharisees gloat.
The priests are exultant.
The soldiers have their chance to show their beastliness.
In the midst of it all, dear Lord, You love.
Was your Mother standing by, weeping?
Her sorrow must have added to yours so much.
You did it all because your Father willed it.
What more was left for You to give?
I never forget that You, such a sorry, beaten, fallen figure
are infinite Majesty and Beauty,
adored by the myriads of mighty angels.
Lord, allow me to walk with You in true humility.
When I feel feeble I come closer to You.
I seem to pray better, to mortify myself more.
But Lord, You rose!
You kept on keeping on—to Calvary.
I want to walk with You.
Inspire me, dear Lord, to make this fall of yours
happen before my eyes, here, now.
I see You as my Father, infinitely loving, wise, powerful, merciful.
In your Eucharistic presence, Jesus,
You keep on keeping on,
remaining with us, no matter how we treat You.
What an example!
Lord, may I follow faithfully.
Give me the grace to imitate your humility, your perseverance.
I want to love for all those who do not love You as they should.

My dear Jesus, I contemplate You as You are,
the King of Glory
clothed with light and beauty as a garment.
You it was who imparted to the sun its brilliance,
who clothed with beauty the flowers of the fields and the
birds of the air.
God from God, Light from Light, true God from true God,
by whom all things were made.
Now I see You stripped naked.
"From the soles of his feet to the top of his head
there is nothing healthy in him; wounds and bruises and swelling sores.
They are not bound up, nor dressed, nor anointed with oil." (Is. 1,6).
What do You see, O infinitely wise Jesus?
You see men whom You created for heaven,
in preference to all the others You might have created.
You see those whom You love with infinite love
rip off your clothes and expose your body,
bruised, torn, bleeding, to the gaze of all.
You know each of them through and through,
their parents, their grand-parents, their families, their children.
You know exactly how guilty each one of them is—
for You long for the salvation of each individual.
"God wills every man to be saved" (1 Tim. 2,4).
Is it too much to believe that when this terrible incident is over,
moved by your grace, these men will think of You,
see You in their minds, remember your patience, nobility and silence?
Were they later members of your Church?
In the Sacred Host You appear to men
stripped of all external grandeur and glory.
In every age your lovers have tried to find fitting adornment for You,
golden monstrances, precious stones, beautiful churches.
How hard it is to raise money to build You a worthy temple
while all around money is being squandered with hardly a thought.
Dear Jesus, You allowed Yourself to be publicly stripped
to atone for the lusts of our race.
I sincerely wish to make reparation by mortifying my flesh.
Lord, with your infinite power You are well able
to halt the tide of lust and immorality in our world.
I beg You, by the love You have for the souls You created for Yourself
to pour forth a torrent of graces now to do just that.

49   THE ELEVENTH STATION

My dear Lord Jesus, You allowed this terrible act.
You are the infinite God.
You willed to die to save men who had rebelled against You.
One drop of your Precious Blood would have been enough.
But You willed not only to die
but to die in the cruellest way possible.
O Mary, my Mother, did You see it all?
Were You not constrained to cry out
"Stop. Do you not know that you are crucifying your God?"?
Those soldiers were your children.
Your Jesus knew them, every detail of their lives.
They only existed because He willed it.
Now as they perform the most terrible deed ever committed
He cries out, "Father, forgive them,
for they know not what they are doing" (Luke, 23,34).
Mother, I cannot begin to imagine your anguish.
Your two loves were here at work,
your love of your dear divine Son
and your love of the will of God.
You knew that He needed not to undergo so much torment.
You knew that He could have avoided those trials,
those humiliations, all that ill-usage, those wicked judgements,
and the shame of being executed like a criminal
on the cruellest of gallows.
You knew, dear Mother, that He wanted to suffer it all
for those who sinned throughout human history.
O what a mystery is here!
The greatest moment of all time.
Man murdering his God, the creature killing his Creator,
the finite destroying the Infinite.
Mary, pray for me.
Pray that with the Holy Spirit's gift of understanding
I shall penetrate by faith deeper and deeper
into the meaning of this infinite mystery.
This moment is preserved in Holy Mass.
Mary, pray that my faith in and devotion to Holy Mass will grow.
Indeed, pray for all your children.
Calvary is a mystery. Holy Mass is a mystery.
But is there not something mysterious, dear Mother,
in the tepidity of your children's appreciation of it all?

O Jesus, help me to contemplate those last hours of yours.
What a profound mystery!
You, King of kings, dying beneath the inscription,
"Jesus of Nazareth, King of the Jews" (Jn. 19,19).
Lord how they mocked You, jeered at You!
But to your defence came a thief,
"This man has done no evil" (Luke 23,41).
I repeat his request in my prayer now,
"Lord, remember me when You come into your kingdom"
(Luke 23,42).
Yes, I acknowledge You as King by conquest.
You suffered terribly in your Body, dear Jesus
but how much more in your spirit!
You looked on your Immaculate Mother.
You understood her unique greatness because You made her.
"Woman, behold your son" (John 19,26).
Lord, say that to her now and point to me.
I renew my consecration to her, all that I am, all that I have.
I know she will give me to You.
You seemed to cry in dereliction to your Father.
You were reciting the inspired words of the psalm,
but those around were too spiritually blind to understand.
Remove from me all spiritual blindness.
May I understand as fully as is possible the inner meaning of
all that is happening?
You cried out, "I thirst" (John 19,28).
Yes, dear Lord, your thirst was for the souls of men.
You gazed across the centuries.
You saw all those You would ever create.
Everyone of them You willed to live in heaven for ever.
Where are your disciples now?
Where is the bold Peter?
Where all those You healed of their infirmities?
Where are those who a few days ago acclaimed You?
The soldier's lance opens your Sacred Heart.
Lord, give me deep, living faith to penetrate its meaning.
How can I hope to understand either your sufferings or your love?
Eternal High Priest, this is your infinite sacrifice.
Your infinite love seized it and preserved it in the Mass.
Oh why, oh why, is not Mass recognised and loved
for the infinitely precious reality it is?

51 THE THIRTEENTH STATION

Lord Jesus, this must be one of the loveliest scenes in history
and one of the most meaningful.
I see your human body
the body of a divine Person,
of God the Son,
dead.
Human life has been sacrificed to atone for sin.
"Greater love than this no man has . . . ." (John 15,13).
O what a terrible return the people You created
have made for your infinite love!
The Immaculate Mother now holds the price of sin.
She sees the shocking wounds,
the tears of the scourges,
the holes of the thorns,
the gashes of the nails,
the rent of the spear.
Every wound of yours is a new wound for her.
She chose to be the Queen of Martyrs
so that she could be Queen of Heaven.
O my dear Mother, Spouse of the Holy Spirit,
endowed as no other creature has been
with the gift of understanding,
you penetrate the deepest meaning of it all.
You have shared by your presence and your prayer
in this infinite act of sacrifice.
By your free consent and from your own pure body
you provided the Priest, the Victim,
and the Precious Blood that was shed.
Still ringing in your ears are the last words He spoke to you,
proclaiming that you are indeed the Mother of Men.
As the blood and water followed the spear being pulled out of his side
you saw the Church mystically signified,
your new child, the mystical Body of your divine Child.
Nothing could add to the infinity of his redeeming love
but you, dear Mother, merited to share in his work of redemption.
By your union with Him you redeemed us with Him.
Mother, take me now into your ever loving arms,
embrace me, kiss me, love me, pray for me,
help me to grow into a worthy image of your Jesus.

Lord, I visit your sealed tomb.
You, God the Son, are dead.
You came into the world in poverty,
born in somebody else's cattle shed.
Your dead body lies in a borrowed tomb.
King of kings, Lord of lords, true God from true God,
You have indeed given your all.
Your blessed Body, the instrument You used to save us
is here only because of the bravery of Joseph and Nicodemus.
Grant that I may always have the courage to stand against the crowd
when I am sure that my cause, my opinions are right.
May I be as devoted to your blessed Body
ever present, but now living, in the tabernacles of our churches.
Grant, good Lord, that I may never abandon You
as Peter and your Apostles did.
Yes, Lord, You died in your human flesh.
May I die to everything that can separate me from You.
Grant that I may never love more
whatever makes me love You less.
I believe, dear Jesus, that at any moment
You could have saved Yourself from this.
You could have come down from the Cross.
But You are dead because You chose to die.
You are here waiting to rise again to triumphant life.
Give me grace to see this for myself.
I know I must die.
How or where or when I do not know.
But at that moment I shall be judged by You,
my tremendous Lover, who died for me.
Grant that when this moment comes
I shall be ready, never having ceased to be your lover.
I accept my death now.
If I have to suffer a severe illness first
with much pain, I offer all to You.
But, dear Lord, I beg You in your mercy help me to die in your love.
Help those who will care for me in my last illness.
Mary, my Mother, you love me as your child.
Your dear Son said, "As long as you did it to one of my least brethren,
You did it to me" (Matt. 25,40).
Mary, dearest Mother, love me as you loved Him.

53 HOLY ABANDONMENT

Lord, I am convinced that the surest way to holiness
is the way of abandonment to your holy will.
Teach me at every moment to learn what You desire,
to will only what You will,
in the way You will it.
I believe that if I succeed in this
I shall give You more glory than by any other way.
Give me grace and strength, Heavenly Father, to live your will,
with liveliest faith, firmest hope and perfect charity.
Fill the vacuum created in my soul caused by
my desire for abandonment
with the permanent spirit of prayer.
I beg for your will,
the will of infinite love and infinite wisdom
to be the master of my life.
Lord, am I wrong in wishing by loving abandonment to your will
to die with You to the world
and to live for your Father?
Teach me to practise abandonment to your will
for its own sake.
Yes, heavenly Father, I long to throw myself blindly
into the loving embrace of your will.
It may be hard; it may bring me suffering;
it may cause me to be misunderstood,
but I know there can be no better way.
My greatest fear is that the love of self may crush me.
If I succeed in completely abandoning myself to You
that can never happen.
You are my infinitely kind Father.
At every moment You take me by my hand.
I rest confidently in my trust of your wise and loving will.
The more I ponder and pray about the way of abandonment
the more convinced I become, loving Father,
that nothing can give me greater freedom, security or peace.
I want to be one of the little ones to whom You reveal your secrets.
Your Son, my Jesus, thanked You for this.
I pray that by living in total abandonment to your holy will
I shall experience the peace and joy of your Holy Spirit
and that all my efforts for good will be more effective.

54 PERFECT TRUST

Yes, Lord, I understand that I should trust You completely.
Help me to detach myself entirely from the things of earth,
from all that seems to be delightful, powerful and illustrious.
My sincere wish is to be able to love You more than anyone or
anything else.
I am convinced that nothing can compare with You.
Enliven my belief in your infinite goodness, your bounty,
your tender mercy, your limitless generosity.
Lord, I wish to be so surrendered to your will
that I am entirely indifferent to health, sickness, comfort,
riches, honour or contempt,
to a long life or a short one.
If You call me to Yourself to-morrow, blessed be your will.
If You will me to live many more years, blessed be your will.
Around me, heavenly Father, I see sin,
the fruits of man's fall.
I believe that You do not will sin
but in your love You permit it.
Abandonment to your will may mean that I suffer from the
sins of others.
Help me to remain tranquil, completely surrendered.
I wish to live completely conformed to your will, Lord.
That is your love. It is your goodness. It is your wisdom.
Grant me the immense grace of abandoning myself
without resisting, without complaining, without seeking comfort.
I believe that the more painful abandonment becomes
so much more meritorious it is.
It is my sharing in the sacrifice of Calvary.
Help me to such a state of abandonment, dear heavenly Father,
that I become one with You
and You become one with me to form me into Yourself.
Your thoughts are far above human thoughts.
I know I must search for your will sometimes in the dark.
What I long for is to place my will as a sacrifice on the altar
and for You to consume it in the fire of your love
so that I will do only what pleases You.
Help me to look for your will everywhere.
I long to be convinced even more firmly
that no enterprise, no ambition, no plan, no design
has any value apart from You.

55   CLOTHED IN HOPE

Heavenly Father, I beg You to clothe me in hope.
I long for the things of the spirit.
Make my hope in You a hope that is really living.
Fire me with such an understanding of the wonders of eternal life
that in their context the things of this world will be valueless.
Yet You, Lord, have made possible
the wonders of the material world
that have been discovered even in my lifetime.
You willed that I should live during the years
when the marvels of the universe have been revealed
to such an extent that men have been filled with awe.
Day after day I hear or read about more scientific progress.
Yet wonderful as all these things are
they are as nothing to the life that awaits me
in the timeless eternity which is my destiny.
If it were possible for me to see together all the most beautiful things
known to man
they would be worthless in comparison with the beauty of eternal life.
Lord, I grieve that the vast majority of those among whom I live
seem to be quite indifferent to eternity.
They are heedless of You.
They seem to be ignorant of the Incarnation of your divine Son.
Calvary has no meaning for them.
Death is a full stop—the end.
God, how can it be?
You made them all for Yourself.
You will them all to be saved
and to come to the knowledge of the truth.
Why do You allow those who are clothed in hope
to be so few, so isolated, regarded as oddities?
The very fact that I want to live in hope
makes me long to make reparation to You
for those who have no hope.
Lord, I pray for them.
Only You can turn their minds to hope.
Strengthen my confidence, good Lord.
Give me a living certitude in the truth of all You have revealed.
You wish to be my eternal possession and beatitude.
But You also wish me to possess You now by charity and grace.
Then, Lord, strengthen my conviction that You invite me
to live in intimate union with You.

I turn to you, Joseph, husband and support of Mary,
Foster-father of God the Son made man.
You were chosen for these unique responsibilities
from amongst all the men God created or might have created.
God knew that you would respond to his choice of you
by immense faith and perfect obedience.
An angel of God revealed to you the mystery of Mary's motherhood
changing your perplexity into joy.
You shared with Mary the anxieties of your flight into Egypt
and those days when Jesus was lost in the Temple.
As head of the Holy Family you held over the God-man
all the rights of a father.
Alone of all men you were the lawful superior of God.
You had to sanctify yourself by governing God.
God chose you, Joseph, to be the guardian
of the greatest treasure on earth, the infant God.
From amongst all you were chosen to be the husband
of the holy Virgin, Mary Immaculate, Mother of God.
Your marriage is the ideal and exemplar of all marriage,
the noblest of them all
for your union was of souls, minds and hearts
as perfect as could be.
Teach me, dear Joseph, to grow in intimacy with Jesus and Mary.
How you must have learned from daily living with them!
I wish to learn from you also the lesson of work.
Prince of contemplatives, you spent your life
as a humble, hardworking, industrious village tradesman.
How can I imprint these lessons firmly on my soul?
You, the greatest ruler of the world,
who ruled God with full authority,
who lived in closest intimacy with God
plied a humble trade in the obscurity of a village cottage.
Teach me that I can be holy in the world as well as in the cloister.
Teach me how to be intimate with Jesus and Mary by constant prayer.
Teach me to act rather than to say,
to do what I ought to do,
when I ought to do it,
as I ought to do it and why I ought to do it
that so doing I shall be brought to the happiness of a death like yours
in the company of Jesus, your God and your Child
and of Mary, your Queen and your wife.

57 MISSION

"Go out into the whole world.
Preach the Gospel to every creature" (Mark 16,15).
This, dear Lord, was your mandate to your Church.
What has happened?
What do You think now, dear Master?
You must be offering to all your children
grace to obey your command.
Why is that grace not effective?
I beg You, Lord, renew in your Church
conviction of what it means to be your Body.
I believe that wherever your members are to be found
they should display your mind and outlook,
your zeal for souls,
your sense of mission.
Lord, I confess to you now
that when I look at your Church
I am sad
because the sense of mission is almost everywhere absent.
You will every man to be saved.
Your Apostle's exhortation rings through the arches of the years,
"Let that mind be in you which was in Christ Jesus" (Phil. 2,5).
We live in the midst of millions of churchless people
who have no knowledge of the treasures of your Church,
who seem to be ignorant of the mysteries of the Incarnation,
Redemption, the Holy Eucharist and eternal life.
Lord, I try to convince those who believe in You
that they must not keep the Faith to themselves.
I know many who attend Mass every Sunday without fail
yet never invite those who stay away to accompany them.
I want to make reparation, dear Lord,
to your Sacred Heart for all those who nowadays
in the interests of a false irenicism
actually oppose organised work to bring about conversions.
Yes, Lord, I am really fearful.
Materialism, irreligion, immorality, godlessness
are growing apace.
They are a terrible threat to our young people.
Dearest Jesus, pour a torrent of grace into your Church
to restore a vital sense of mission
for that seems to be the only way of making the Church
the militant, converting, love-sharing society You mean it to be.

My God, to-day I have been thinking about penance.
I realise that receiving the Sacrament of Penance
should help me grow in perfection.
I want to contemplate it and appreciate it in the light of faith.
Lord, increase my faith.
Inspire me always to see your divine Son, Jesus, in the person of
my confessor.
May I kneel at his feet as I would kneel at the feet of Jesus.
May I confide in him as I would in Jesus.
May I heed his advice as I would the advice of Jesus.
May I approach him with the same confidence with which I would
approach Jesus.
May I use confession in the spirit of love.
May I reject even the slightest attachment to sin.
May I arouse within me sentiments of true sorrow
not only for my sins but also for my failure to be holy.
May I approach each confession as if it were to be the last of my life,
an immediate preparation to meet You, my eternal Judge.
Lord, enlighten my soul so that I can examine myself
with true humility and greatest sincerity,
with a spirit that is serene and impartial.
Give me your help so that I may be truly sorry
for my faults and for my failure to seek perfection.
May my spirit of repentance be intense enough
to increase your grace to help me to stride onwards towards ever
greater perfection.
Lord God, I long for sorrow and repentance.
Help me, therefore, to contemplate your goodness and mercy.
Help me to appreciate fully the love and sufferings of Jesus.
Help me to recognise the monstrous ingratitude of the sinner
to You, so good a Father, who have conferred such
great benefits on me.
I believe that the grace of intense, perfect contrition
is your gift, O God, and can be sought only by prayer.
Therefore, I try to humble myself before your divine majesty,
to implore this gift through the intercession of Mary, my sinless Mother.
Dear Lord, every time I go to confession may I make a resolution
that is clear, concrete and energetic
to use every possible means to avoid sin and advance in virtue.
Lord, help me to achieve all these desires.
May I use the gift of your Sacrament to grow daily nearer to You.

59   CONFESSION

Lord Jesus, I examine myself in your presence about confession.
I am always too proud.
Help me to recognise my many weaknesses
and to confess them very frankly.
I am afraid love of self is deep-rooted in me
and far removed from true humility of heart.
You know how sincerely I long to make my regular confessions
instruments of my sanctification.
Grant that I may never be afraid of humiliating myself
before my confessor.
May I never try to make my faults less evil than they are.
May I never try to excuse rather than to accuse myself.
I beg you, dear Lord, to move those to whom I confess
to help me on the way to perfection.
May I never use the Sacrament of Reconciliation
without being truly sorry for my sins, my failures, my shortcomings.
I am convinced, dear Lord, of the value of frequent confession.
I have read about many of your Saints
who believed in even daily confession.
Help me to keep up the practice myself.
Pour your graces into your Church
so that the practice of frequent confession may grow again.
Raise up priests who will convince their people
that frequent confession is one of the most efficacious means
of advancing in perfection.
But, dear Lord, before that can come about
your children must be urged to desire perfection,
to understand the meaning and value of true holiness.
Grant that many more of your children, heavenly Father,
will come to understand the precious effects of frequent confession.
May they long for your Precious Blood to fall on them
to purify and sanctify them.
May they come to appreciate the meaning of sacramental grace.
May they think with the Saints and with the Church
and always recognise how precious frequent confession really is.
Grant that I may persevere in going to confession frequently,
always for your honour and glory,
for my own sanctification, my peace and my consolation,
to receive greater light concerning your ways, O Jesus,
and to increase the power of my soul to overcome temptation
and the courage to fulfil perfectly all my duties.

c

O God, You know how firmly I believe in You.
I ask something more of You.
Fill me with the gift of understanding
so that I shall begin to be aware of what my belief should mean.
I am overcome by the contemplation of your attributes.
All of them are equal to Yourself.
They are infinite, without limits.
I am filled with wonder at the thought of your immensity.
You know everything.
You act in all beings.
You are substantially present in all things and in all places.
But your immensity means that You are immeasurable.
You must be present in places and things which do not exist.
You are entirely everywhere.
You are wholly in every place.
You are wholly without place.
You are not contained or held in place.
You are able to be present in all possible things.
Help me not only to believe
but to understand
what St. Paul said to the men of Athens:
"He is not far from everyone of us,
for in Him we live and move and are" (Acts, 17,27).
The heavens of heavens cannot contain You (II Paral. 6,18).
The mightiest wonders of science,
the latest discoveries of this age of wonders,
cannot exhaust You.
The farthest star, the most distant planet can be measured
but not You, O God.
The wonders of science exceed our powers of imagination.
You, God, infinitely surpass all of them.
You encompass everything but You cannot be encompassed.
Your being permits no limitation, even limitation of space.
O God, help me to understand
in so far as my poor limited mind can understand.
You, limitlessly immeasurable and immense,
became a baby in the womb of one whom You created.
You hide Yourself under the appearance of bread.
You become the food of my soul.

61 SOURCE OF ALL GOOD

O God, how rarely we think deeply about You.
How few of us spend time reading and studying,
trying to understand what You have revealed to us about Yourself.
You inspired the author of Tobit to write,
"Take advantage of every opportunity
to praise the Lord your God.
Ask Him to make You prosper
in whatever you set out to do.
He is the source of all good things" (Tobit 4,19).
Lord, remind me to be faithful to this teaching.
I do not praise You nearly as much or as often or as fervently
as I should.
I forget your presence.
I fear I do not even take You for granted.
I must call upon You for every good I need.
Above all, Lord, I beg You to give me goodness.
For your sake I want to be holy.
I owe that to You.
I must be just one tiny jot in all that your love has made.
Because I came from You I must be good.
Every good I can wish for comes from You.
I am afraid to think of my needs.
They are too many.
You know them all.
In your love pour into my being
everything You know is good for me,
everything You know will lead me to love You more.
I am so desperately proud,
so foolishly self-sufficient.
You see me, Lord, as I really am.
Help me to see myself as You see me.
Force my poor will which is so centred in myself
to turn towards You,
to become absorbed in You,
magnetised by You.
You alone are worthy of all I can give.
Fire my whole being with this conviction.
Compel me to make You the very centre of my life,
my thoughts, my longings, my loves.

62   THE GOODNESS OF GOD

O God, the finite minds of your creatures
can never fully understand the infinite nature of your attributes.
I ponder now your goodness.
You are not only good, but goodness itself—unlimited, unbounded,
immeasurable.
To Moses You, O Lord, cried out,
"I the Lord am a God
who is full of compassion and pity,
who is not easily angered
and who shows great love and faithfulness" (Exod. 34,6).
Yes, Lord, I want to adore the very abundance of your goodness.
So often I pray the inspired words of the Psalmist,
"How wonderful are the good things
You keep for those who honour You!
Everyone knows how good You are,
how securely You protect those who trust You.
You hide them in the safety of your presence
from the plots of men;
in a safe shelter You hide them" (Ps. 31,19).
When I try to contemplate the good things
You have kept for me
I do not know where to begin.
The litany is endless.
You made me.
You could have made another
who You knew would be holier than I
but You chose to make me.
I cannot hope to count all the good things I owe to You.
I shall pause to ponder them now in my prayer
but express them, list them, I cannot.
I praise You, Lord, for them all.
I cannot thank You enough.
Help me to repay your goodness
by being wholly faithful to You.
I know very well that only perfection is worthy of You.
I wish to be perfect according to the capacity You give me.
What that capacity is You alone know.
Of myself, alone, I cannot take the least step forward to perfection.
I depend entirely on You.
So help me, good Lord.

63 THE OVERWHELMING VISION OF GOD

I believe, O God, that as I pray now I am in You.
The thought overwhelms me.
Why, over the years, have I been so slow in grasping
the meaning of all You have revealed about Yourself?
Help me now to understand.
Thousands of years ago Joshua encouraged his people,
"You will know," he said, "that the living God is among you"
(Joshua 3,10).
Lord, I believe that You are the same living God.
I believe that You are everywhere
with all your infinite attributes.
I believe it, Lord, but how can I understand it?
I regret that so few of your creatures seem to try to understand it.
Lord, You can do all things.
Move our race to recognise and realise and understand
that You, the living God, are among us.
Once You inspired Isaiah to beg the people to listen to You.
He reminded them that You are all powerful and were saying,
"I will purify you in the way metal is refined
and will remove all your impurity" (Isaiah 1,25).
Lord, is this true?
Why do You seem to stand apart and let godlessness rule?
Are the tragedies of our day your punishments for sin?
Why, then, do You not make us realise this?
Why are the voices of your servants unheard?
Why does the world rush on its way to disaster?
Lord, I know that You are holy, almighty, eternal,
the universal King, the Lord of the ages,
the God of the universe, the God of truth,
the infinite Lover.
Why then, I pray You, do You allow this race You love
to distance its conduct ever further away from your law?
You teach, Lord, through your Church.
Raise up in your Church people who will influence the world for good.
Give us Saints whose voices will be heard
and whose message will be accepted everywhere.
When You seem to remain apart
men live as if You do not exist.
Lord, I am so small, so powerless.
I seem to be able to do so very little.
You can do everything.

64   LOVE OF GOD

I believe, O God, that You are love, infinite love.
I try to bring home to myself the meaning of infinite love.
I think of every kind of love,
every expression of love.
I think of all the human love there has ever been,
love of husbands for wives and wives for husbands,
of parents for children and of children for parents,
of children, relatives and friends for one another.
I think of all the love shown in works of compassion and service.
I think of the love of patriotism.
I add the love of all good people for You, O God,
the love which burned in the hearts of all the Saints.
I try to comprehend the love of Mary's Immaculate Heart.
I count also the love of all the countless angels
as they sing their hymns in praise of You.
I know that if I add all these loves together,
or even multiply them by each other if that were possible,
the sum total would be as nothing
when compared with You, Lord, who are love.
My mind is inundated, flooded, overwhelmed by this thought.
You, infinite Love, are everywhere.
It is in You, Love, that everything happens.
It has always been so.
How long our race has existed I know not.
For how long You have been adored by the angelic choirs
I cannot begin to contemplate.
But, everywhere and always, through these countless years
angels and men have loved.
They have sinned, too.
When the angels rebelled and became devils
they did it in your love.
Hell exists within your love.
All that so disgusts me to-day
all that has ever been done against your will
has been done in your love
because You, God, are Love
and You are everywhere.
Lord, I believe.
Unfold to me the consequences of all these truths.

65   THE WAYS OF GOD

"This God, how perfect are his deeds!"
sung the Psalmist (Ps. 18,30).
Lord, I am grieved that so few of your children
seem to contemplate the wonder of your works.
The revelations of science become more astounding every day.
They are all your works.
Your children use the faculties You gave them
to discover the prodigies of your creation.
In your presence, Lord, I ponder the inspired words of St. Paul,
"How great are God's riches!
How deep are his wisdom and knowledge!
Who can explain his decisions?
Who can understand his ways?
For all things were created by Him
and all things exist through Him and for Him" (Rom. 11, 35-36).
In the years that You have permitted me to live, Lord,
the feats of men of science have been astounding.
How sad it is that those wonders
do not lead those who discover them
to You who created and designed them!
Lord, I adore You in the wonders of your creation.
I marvel at the prodigies of your ways.
Your beloved disciple described your victorious children singing,
"Lord, God Almighty,
how great and wonderful are your deeds!
King of the nations,
how right and true are your ways!
Who will not stand in awe of You, Lord?
Who will refuse to declare your greatness?
You alone are holy.
All nations will come
and worship You,
because your just actions are seen by all" (Rev. 15, 3-4).
O Lord, I beg You use your love and your power
to turn the minds of thinkers and scientists to You.
Make them ponder the sources and origins
of all they discover and study.
Lead them thus, O Lord, to You.
"All You do is strange and wonderful.
I know it with all my heart" (Ps. 139,14).

O God, because You are perfection You must be infinite beauty.
The very thought confounds me.
You are Spirit, Lord.
Your beauty is not material; it is not temporal.
Dare I compare it with the beauties of your creation?
For I marvel at the beauty of nature,
at the vision of the snow-capped mountains
set against the blue of the sky.
I am thrilled by the towering waves of the sea,
by the roar and turbulence of swiftly flowing water.
I quite fail to contemplate the glorious colours of the birds
and the fishes.
I try but never succeed to appreciate
the sweet beauty of music and all harmony and song.
I admire the manifold fragrance and
the colours and design of trees and flowers.
I am stirred by the beauty of poetry and literature.
I am astounded by the vision of the stars at night.
But your beauty, O God, is such that
no picture, no word, no music can express.
You are every perfection without limit.
For centuries men have written about your attributes.
They have tried to translate your glory into music,
your majesty into words and pictures.
But I know the task is impossible.
I pray that your thinking creatures will learn about You
from the beauties of your creation.
When they add them all together
they are less than nothing compared with You.
All the beauty in them,
all of it combined
in millions upon millions of elements in creation
must be first in You.
But yours, O God, is spiritual beauty,
beauty infinitely exceeding
the noblest thought of men or of angels.
Lord, I bow in humble adoration.
I thank You for allowing me to contemplate your beauty
and beg that I may reflect it in my own
thoughts and words and deeds.

67   THE GIFTS OF GOD

O God, You inspired your Wise Man to proclaim,
"Everything comes from the Lord;
success and failure, poverty and wealth, life and death.
Wisdom, understanding, knowledge of the Law,
love and the doing of good deeds—
all these come from the Lord . . . .
The Lord's gifts to religious people
are gifts that endure" (Sir. 11, 14-17).
How can one list all your gifts?
My whole being came from You.
Every minute of my life has come from You.
My health and sleep and rest,
my food, my family,
every circumstance of my day
have come from You.
I remember the inspired words of St. Paul,
"Command those who are rich in the things of this life
not to be proud
but to place their hope, not in such uncertain things as riches,
but in God, who generously gives us everything for our enjoyment."
And also, "God will supply all your needs" (Phil. 4,19; 1 Tim. 6,17).
But, Lord, how much greater are your spiritual gifts!
"God loved the world so much
that He gave his only Son
so that everyone who believes in Him
may not die but have eternal life" (John 3,16).
You, Jesus, told us of your gift of the Holy Spirit.
"Bad as you are, you know how to give good things to your children.
How much more, then, will the Father in heaven
give the Holy Spirit to those who ask Him?" (Luke 11,13).
Lord, I thank You for grace, wisdom and repentance,
for faith, peace and rest,
for a new heart and mind,
for glory, eternal life and infinitely more.
You have given me your Church
with all its certain guidance and consolations,
your Saints for my example and encouragement,
and your own blessed Mother to be my Mother too.
Lord, I can never thank You enough.

68   FOR GOD

My loving, living heavenly Father,
life for me means to be united with You,
to live in intimacy with You,
to give glory to You
and so to win grace for the whole Church.
I will, with all my being,
to live in the atmosphere of your presence.
You live in me.
I live in You.
Move me, Lord, to strive constantly
after more perfect union,
union by love, union by prayer,
and union through the total giving of myself to You.
Honestly, Lord, I do not wish to live for myself.
I wish to live wholly for your glory
and thus for the salvation of all men.
I wish my whole life to be dominated
by my efforts to be one with You.
I will my every activity to be directed towards it.
But I know this must all be your gift.
Of myself I can do nothing.
I cannot take one step forward towards holiness.
So, loving Father, give me this longing
for intimate union with You
for the needs of your Church and the sanctification of mankind.
Let me never sacrifice my mission of prayer
for some passing contact with the world.
Keep me, Lord, ever looking towards You.
I want You to occupy all the room in my soul.
I want You to live alone within me
in the sense that no other love must displace your love.
Protect me, loving Father, from anything
which will turn me from You
or lessen my love for You.
It is You who must fill all my capacity for loving.
I know You will only give Yourself to me
as I give myself to You.
Make the surrender of myself to You
just as perfect as You desire it to be.

69   MY GOD, MY ALL

Loving Father, ever living eternal God,
I wish to open all my heart and will and soul to You.
You are the Sun which will warm me.
You are the Light which will enable me to see.
You are the Power by which I progress.
You are the strength by which I resist temptation.
I wish to attain the state in which I can say with truth:
only one thing matters for me, and that is your will.
That will is your love, your goodness, your wisdom.
Through love of your will
I wish to plunge deeper and deeper into your love.
Help me to make my loving abandonment perfect,
to surrender lovingly to all You wish for me.
Lift me to a condition in which I shall count as nothing
tiredness, humiliations, repugnancies
and all that touches my self-centredness.
I look forward to the day when, with your help, I can say,
"Jesus, my God, You are really my All.
I am yours and You are all to me.
I give myself to You
because You have given Yourself to me."
I know that the more completely I abandon myself to You
the more You will give to me.
Yes, Lord, I am convinced that this and only this
is the way to peace . . .
Lack of surrender means lack of peace.
You are calling me, Father, from morning till night.
Teach me to look always to You.
Guide me with your loving wisdom.
I know I shall experience joy and sorrow,
trial and success, dryness and consolation.
But, good Lord, make me feel your touch.
Open my mind to your inspiration.
Speak to me; lead me.
Give me the one thing I most desire—
absolute, total faithfulness to You.
Teach me how to make my whole life
an example of surrender and fidelity,
of humility and love.

"I am who am; this is my name forever" (Exod. 3,14).
Thus You revealed Yourself, O God, to Moses.
"Supreme Being"—how can I comprehend the meaning of it?
This is your foremost perfection.
This distinguishes You, O God, from creatures
This is your very essence—to be the eternally subsistent Being—
with no beginning and no end—
self-existing; You find the cause of your Being in Yourself.
In You Being is a kind of sea of subsistence, shoreless, infinite.
Of Yourself You proclaim, "I am He who is."
To me You say, "You are he who is not."
With the Psalmist I pray,
"My substance is as nothing before You;
I am withered like grass.
But You, O Lord, endure for ever" (Pss. 38,6; 101, 12-13).
I contemplate the variety of creatures.
Each of them has received Being from You.
How wonderful, how infinitely great, wise, good and loving
You are to create such a galaxy
from the highest angel and the brightest star
to the humblest insect.
But You are the cause of your own Being.
Your creatures exist only so long as You maintain them in existence.
You, infinite God, are your own existence.
By your very nature You possess Being.
You do not receive it from anyone.
Creatures, even the greatest of them, are limited in every respect—
in being and intelligence, in vitality, strength and ability.
But You, O God, are infinite Being,
with no limits of any kind, with all power and virtue.
Only You can communicate life, give existence.
You are life.
You chose in your infinite freedom to create me.
I owe everything I am, everything I have,
the time, the place, the circumstances of my birth to You.
When I consecrate myself to You
I am simply recognising the state of affairs which already exists.
I must live for You.
Living for You is living for life.
Help me, Lord, to be really and truly all yours.

71   ALL ONE IN GOD

God, I profess fervently my belief.
You are the one infinitely perfect Being.
You possess every perfection, without defect, without limit.
You are goodness, beauty, wisdom, justice, mercy, power.
All these perfections are one with your Being.
They are in reality but one infinite perfection.
Your goodness is your beauty.
Your goodness and your beauty are your wisdom.
Your goodness, your beauty and your wisdom are your justice.
These four and every other perfection are your mercy.
All your limitless perfections are one.
In You there is just one absolute unity, no multiplicity.
To speak adequately of You, O God, enough words do not exist
but You are not many things.
You are the one Being, par excellence.
You are One in the Trinity of your Persons,
one in the multiplicity of your perfections,
one in the immense variety of your works,
one in your thought and will and love.
Lord, I long to reflect in my life your unity.
I really wish to see everything in You,
the people around me, my work, my interests,
my thinking, my speaking, the whole of my living.
I want to be wholly yours,
a kingdom in which Your rule is absolute;
not a kingdom divided in itself.
Reveal to me ever more deeply
the meaning of the name You made known to Moses.
I wish to join myself to You
who contain, indeed are, all the perfections of Being.
My being finds nobility and strength
through being united with your Being.
You alone can satisfy the deepest longings of my spirit.
I cannot find satisfaction apart from You.
"O Lord, my God, how great You are;
You are clothed with majesty and glory;
You cover Yourself with light.
I will proclaim your greatness,
my God and my King.
I will thank You for ever and ever" (Pss. 102, 104, 145).

O God, I praise and adore your greatness.
In You is nothing that is composite.
I am composed of body and soul.
In You there are no quantitative parts.
In You there is no matter.
You are pure spirit.
You made the angels pure spirits
but because You made them
their essence is distinct from their existence.
No angel can exist unless You called him to life.
You, O God, are infinitely superior to the highest angel.
Your essence exists of itself.
You are the one and only eternally subsistent Being.
Inspire me to understand You,
not composed of goodness, beauty, wisdom and justice
but being at the same time the one
infinitely good, beautiful, wise and just Being.
In You substance and quality are one.
Your limitless attributes are your very substance.
In You being is not distinct from action.
You are pure act,
the act of an infinite intellect which always subsists
and embraces all truth.
At the same time You are the act of a will
which always subsists and desires good.
In You thoughts do not succeed one another.
You are one, single, immutable, subsistent thought,
which comprehends all truth.
Likewise, in You there are not separate acts of the will
which follow one another
but one single act, perfect, immutable,
always willing good with an infinitely pure intention.
If it permits evil, it does so only with a view to greater good.
O infinite God move me to live with perfect simplicity.
I wish to act only to please You.
Let this holy desire dominate my life.
My wish is that in the multiplicity of my acts
there will be perfect simplicity and profound unity.
Let me not halt between love of myself and love of You
but cause me to walk on one road only,
the straight road of duty, of your will and good pleasure.

73   GOD UNCHANGEABLE

"Every good gift and every perfect present
comes from heaven; it comes down from God,
the Creator of the heavenly lights
who does not change" (James, 1,17).
Only in You, because you are infinite
is there no change or shadow of alteration.
In You, O God, there is no limit, no beginning, no end.
In You every attribute, every perfection, is infinite.
Imprint in the very centre of my being
this deep, vivid conviction of your timelessness.
You were in the past; You are in the present; You will be in the future.
You were, because You never were not.
You will be, because You will never cease to exist.
You are because You always exist.
In You, Lord, nothing is past, nothing is future.
All is timelessly present.
I believe that You are eternal
because You have, indeed are, full, perfect, interminable life,
with no change,
which subsists by itself,
with infinite power, vigour and perfection,
interminable, with no beginning and no end,
never susceptible to succession or progress.
You are the very fullness of infinite life all at once.
You cannot change because You are by nature
limitless perfection.
You cannot lose anything of your perfect attributes.
You cannot add anything to them.
You are always the same,
never young, never old.
Your life is one eternal day,
with no yesterday, no to-morrow.
You see my life in your eternal timelessness.
Every thought, word, deed and omission of mine
are always present to You,
those that are past, those present now to me
and those of my future.
Good God, I remember this truth as I pray now.
Ensure that I remember it at every moment.
You see me now at every moment that makes up my life.
May I never forget your timeless presence.

My dear God, if I were to write every day for ever
I could never describe adequately the beauties of nature.
I have seen the rich glory of the rising sun
and the red beauty of its setting over the silver sea.
I have seen the allure of snow-capped peaks,
the fairness of the fields of the rolling countryside,
the crystal effervescence of the rushing stream,
the virgin white of untrodden snow,
the myriad silver points of the milky way.
Yes, Lord, immense beauty indeed
but only a tiny fraction of all that can delight
the human eye or ear or mind.
I think, too, of the immense invisible world,
of the myriads of mighty spirits untramelled by limitations of flesh.
Am I not right, O God, in supposing
that the beauty of your invisible creation
must far surpass the beauty we are able to see or hear?
How, then, can I hope to comprehend your beauty,
O great, unlimited Creator of all?
You must possess the beauty of your visible and invisible creation.
Within your infinite Being
You must possess beauties
You have never communicated to any creature,
which are proper to You alone.
O Lord, I imagine the impossible—
that You are an infinite mirror
reflecting all at once all created beauty.
I thank You dear Lord for even allowing me
to think as I pray of your beauty
so infinitely indescribable because You contain in Yourself
all the perfections of your entire creation as well as your own.
Words do not exist with which I can tell You all I mean.
O my God, You are the brightness of eternal light.
You are a spotless mirror of infinite majesty.
You are a paradise of all delights.
Your beauty is such that it perfectly satisfies your
infinite capacity for happiness.
Open the eyes of my spirit, Lord, that they may be entranced
by your immeasurable, indescribable beauty.
This is a vision which awaits me
as I emerge from this valley of darkness.
Lord, grant that I may never cease to thirst for You.

75   TEMPTATION

My dear Loving Master, I know You permit me to be tempted.
You must allow it for my spiritual good.
Jesus. You permitted Satan to tempt You. "The Spirit led Jesus into
the desert to be tempted by the devil" (Matt.4,1).
You allowed the Pharisees and Sadducees to tempt You.
"Some Pharisees and Sadducees who came to Jesus
wanted to tempt Him" (Matt.16,1).
Even Simon Peter tried to tempt You.
But You replied, "Get away from me, Satan!
You are an obstacle in my way,
because these thoughts of yours do not come from God
but from men" (Matt.17,23).
The inspired writer of the Letter to the Hebrews reminds me,
"He had to become like his brothers in every way,
in order to be their faithful and merciful High Priest
in his service to God,
so that the people's sins might be forgiven.
And now He can help those who are tempted
because He Himself was tempted and suffered (Heb.1, 17-18).
Lord Jesus, You were tempted because You willed it.
I am tempted when I do not will it . . .
I cannot hope to live without temptation.
I can never escape from the struggle to overcome it.
I believe that the struggle is the price of eternal life.
"Happy is the person who remains faithful under trial,
because when he succeeds in passing such a test,
he will receive as his reward the life
which God has promised to those who love Him" (James 1,12).
I know that You, O Lord, always offer to those who are tempted
grace sufficient to overcome the temptation.
"God keeps his promise, and He will not allow you to be tested
beyond your power to remain firm;
at the time you are put to the test
He will give you strength to endure it
and so provide you with a way out" (1 Cor.10,13).
May I never fail in my trust of You, O Lord.
I know that You are always with me.
Remind me when temptation comes to turn my thoughs to You.
May I flee away from temptations against faith and purity.
You say, "I will save those who love me
and will protect those who acknowledge me as Lord . . .
When they are in trouble I will be with them . . .
I will save them" (Ps.91, 15-16).

O God, You are rightly adored
as Most High, seated above the Seraphim.
Yet in You we live and move and have our being.
You probe the incomprehensible with the clarity of your vision
and yet I could not be nearer to You.
Truly, everything is open and naked to your eyes.
I adore You as all wise, all powerful, all holy, all love.
I know You made everything outside Yourself.
The more I try to contemplate You as You are,
in all your infinite perfections,
the more I want to love You.
I feel that if it were possible
I would like to run off to a solitary place
where I could do nothing but contemplate You,
adore You, love You and live for You.
But that is not possible.
In your infinite love You created me at a certain moment.
You placed me in a certain place.
You designed the circumstances in which I have lived.
You have given me so much.
Your greatest instruction to me is that I must love You
with all that I am and all that I have.
You reveal to me that in loving You
is virtue, peace, sweetness, merit, freedom, happiness
and all that is truly good.
I cannot love You without knowing You.
That is why I beg You to endow me with the power
to know You with full comprehension
as well as is possible for my limited sinful being.
Nothing is as good as You,
nothing as perfect, nothing as beautiful.
Yet You bid me call You "Father".
What more can I do, loving Father, to know You more fully?
With my bodily senses I experience material things.
You are the infinite Creator of them all.
Am I longing for the impossible
when I beg to have within my poor being
an image of your majesty which surpasses comprehension?
Lord, I beg You enlighten me.

77   LONGING FOR GOD

O my God, your first and greatest commandment to me is
that I should love You,
with all my heart and mind and soul and strength.
I want to spend my whole life doing just this,
But how can I love unless I first know?
And how can I who am so finite and limited
know You who are infinite and unlimited?
How can I know You when I cannot see You?
Nothing can be in my mind which is not first in my senses.
How can You, Lord, who are infinite enter my mind in that way?
How can I form an image of You who are infinite?
No created mind can reach the ultimate reaches of Your substance
because it has none, Lord.
You are infinitely above every created nature.
How can I adequately contemplate You,
Who are eternal in duration, infinite in power, supreme in authority?
How can I contemplate your being,
Which neither began in time nor terminates in the world?
No thinker around me,
no philosopher alive,
is able to comprehend the soul by which I live,
Which is made to your image and likeness.
How then can I ever hope to arrive at a knowledge,
of your sovereign and incomprehensible nature, O Lord?
Must I desist in my endeavour?
Do you wish me to live without the knowledge
which is the beginning of love?
Deep down I am more than convinced,
that there is no wisdom save in knowing You.
Nor is there any rest apart from You.
There are no true delights except those experienced
in gazing on your beauty, Lord.
Yet, am I not right in trying to know a little about infinite things,
than in trying to know much, however clearly about lowly things?
Of course I who am finite cannot know completely
You who are infinite.
But at least I long to know all I am able to know,
and to love all I know.
I thank You, Lord, for this.
Help me by your grace.

My Lord God, I thank You,
for revealing to us the marvels of your grandeur.
What I am able to to know arouses in me,
love and reverence for your holy name.
I thank you for your gift of faith.
I thank you for all I am able to learn about You in the Scriptures.
I thank You, too, for allowing your beauty,
to shine forth in the perfections of all You have created.
The whole visible world is like a mirror You hold before me,
in which I am able to contemplate your beauty
The perfection of their making reveals them
as so many illuminated letters,
which declare your beauty and your wisdom.
How many, how innumerable they are.
In them I see reflected your many perfections.
Your beauty, your strength, your grandeur,
your wisdom, your charity, your sweetness, your providence.
Your creation is like a mighty choir of countless voices
proclaiming in wonderful harmony, the greatness of your glory.
Every leaf, every flower, every bird, every fish
displays the marvels of your wisdom and power.
Why is our race so silent?
Why are not voices raised in their thousands to acclaim You?
Why do we not know the Master through his works?
O my God, everything in this universe is a letter from You.
Living creatures are living letters
in which you tell us about Yourself.
They speak to us of your wisdom, your grandeur, your love.
What immense love prompted You to make
so many wonderful things for us.
Why do millions of intelligent men gaze on your works,
delight in them, praise them, paint them
and yet forget You the infinitely loving Maker?
My dear Lord, do not permit me to be so blind.
Pour the light of your Holy Spirit into my mind
so that I may see You revealed in the world around me.
May I never cease to love, adore and thank You.
Open my mind to recognise and adore your wisdom,
your omnipotence, your beauty, your goodness, your providence.
Guide me by that providence,
teach me by your truth,
give life to my soul with your love.

79   THE RISEN LORD

O Lord, gloriously risen and loving,
give me deep faith and incisive understanding
of the meaning of your divinity.
Let living faith be on my lips
and in my heart.
Lord, I believe that faith is the foundation of holiness.
I believe that love is the heart of holiness.
I believe that true holiness is based
on the proclamation that You, Jesus, are the Lord.
I pray to understand all the implications of this.
Your Holy Spirit inspired Paul to write.
"The full content of the divine nature lives in Christ" (Col. 1,19).
I think of You, therefore my Jesus
in your mother's womb,
as a toddler and a little boy,
as an adolescent and a teenager,
as a young man in the village,
as an apprentice carpenter,
as joining the dusty battalions of the workers of the world.
You became the teacher because You are the Truth.
In the few words that are recorded as spoken by You is more wisdom
than in all the literature of the world.
You are wisdom, so it must be so.
You chose what to say.
You chose what not to say.
You founded a Church.
So, Lord, in that living Church,
your Body, your other self
the "full content of the divine nature"
must somewhere be found.
Show me Lord how to find it
in the authority of the Pope and the bishops,
in the life to which we are born in baptism,
in the Holy Eucharist, your living Self,
in all the other Sacraments and the Liturgy.
O Christ, You are alive.
In You, my God, I live and move and am.
I adore You, I thank You,
I trust You, I surrender myself to You.
O praised forever be your glorious Resurrection.

The Blood of Jesus was made precious enough to redeem us
by the godhead of the Eternal Trinity.
"Eternal Trinity, you are like a deep sea
in which the more I seek, the more I find;
the more I find the more I seek You".
Lord, the more I contemplate your limitless attributes
the more I hunger and thirst for You.
You are the Light.
In You the Light, enable me to see You ever more clearly.
Make me always dissatisfied with what I find in You.
Excite in me a longing for more.
Holy Spirit, intensify your gift of understanding in me.
May I discover You more and more in the beauty of your creation.
May I understand how I am your image.
I am your living image by the gift
of your power, your wisdom and your love.
Holy Spirit, You proceed eternally from the Father and the Son.
You have prepared me for this longing for divine love.
Give me the will to love You ever more.
Eternal Trinity, you are in love with the beauty of your creation.
I am a new creation,
made new in the Blood of God the Son.
O eternal Trinity, you are an abyss, a deep sea
yet You come to live in me.
You have given your Infinite Self to me.
What a mystery! What greater could You give?
You are a fire ever burning, never consumed.
Consume in your heart all the self-loving of my soul.
Consume my pride, my vanity, my bigheadedness.
Burn away all my egotism, my self-admiration, my conceit.
You are infinite goodness, supreme, blessed, incomprehensible.
You are beauty beyond all beauty.
You are wisdom beyond all wisdom.
You are love beyond all love.
Magnetise me, Lord, by the contemplation
of all your infinite attributes.
Arouse in me a never ceasing spiritual hunger.
Continue to feed it by pouring into my soul
all the gifts of your most Holy Spirit.

81   MARY IMMACULATE

O Mary, my dearest, sweetest Mother,
I want to talk with you about your Immaculate Conception.
What a unique, what a wonderful privilege!
It was a fitting prelude to all your other privileges.
When did you realise your sinlessness?
When did you understand that you were the woman of whom God
spoke to Satan after Adam's fall?
In your days in the temple did you read the Book of Genesis?
The Holy Spirit who inspires the Scriptures is your Spouse!
Or did your divine Son first tell you of it?
Did you talk with Him about the sin of Adam and Eve?
Mother, I know that that first prophecy of redemption
came from the lips of God Himself.
It was He who foretold the complete enmity
which would exist between you and Satan.
Did Jesus ever talk to you about the joys of the angels
when they saw your soul
the first since Eve's
coming sinless from the creative hand of God?
Did you know before Gabriel saluted you
that you were full of grace?
Did your divine Child ever talk to you about your unique holiness
about how you were adorned with all the gifts of the Holy Spirit?
Mother, did you meditate on your sinlessness?
Did you know that by God's power
you were protected from every imperfection?
Mother mine, I want to love you
in a way proportionate to your absolute sinlessness
and perfection of virtues.
Your enmity with sin gives you unique power with your Son.
You canot suffer now in heaven.
But what do you think of the world of my day,
a world which has lost its sense of sin?
Have you already suffered for all this?
Was your grief at the never ending sinfulness of man
included in the sorrow of your years on earth?
Mother, pray that I may regard sin as you do
and, with you as my teacher, learn to love your Son.

O my dearest Mother, reigning in heaven,
I have to turn to the words of the Saints
to find titles which express your Immaculate Conception.
You are a Lily among thorns,
a Land Wholly Intact,
Always Blessed,
Free from all Contagion of Sin,
Unfading Tree,
Fountain ever Clear,
the one and only daughter not of Death but of Life,
offspring not of Wrath but of Grace,
Unimpaired and ever Unimpaired,
Holy and Stranger to all Stain of Sin,
More Comely than Comeliness itself
More Holy than Sanctity,
Alone, Holy Who, excepting God, is Higher than All,
By Nature more Beautiful, More Graceful
and More Holy than the Cherubim and Seraphim themselvess
and the Whole Host of Angels.
My dear mother, obtain for me
the grace to understand these marvellous titles.
They prove to the whole world that
of you alone among holy men and women
can it be said that the question of sin does not arise.
God's infinite holiness demanded that
He would not dwell in and be
formed in his human body
of one who had even for a moment
been stained by the sin
He became man to conquer.
This privilege of yours, O my Mother,
is due to the infinite merits of your divine Son.
You were redeemed by Him
but in a most perfect way.
Your Immaculate Conception reminds the whole world
of the esteem it must have of spiritual goods.
It is the great sign of your victory over sin
and over the devil.
Mother dear, obtain for me a hatred of sin and a love of virtue
that are worthy of you.

83   THE MOST PERFECT MOTHER

I turn to you, the Immaculate Mother of God and my mother.
I beg you obtain for me
a little understanding of your sublime holiness.
To you, God the Father gave his only-begotten Son,
the Son who is equal to the Father and begotten by Him,
Whom He loves with the Infinite Love
that is Himself.
So the Father willed that you and He
would both be able to call Jesus Son.
He the divine Son, chose to make you his Mother.
It was from you that the Holy Spirit
willed and brought it about that
God the Son should be conceived and born,
God the Son, that is, from whom the Holy Spirit proceeds.
I believe, O Mary, that you were conceived free from all stain of
original sin
because you were predestined to be the Mother of God.
Your soul had to reflect in its beauty the holiness of your Son.
How can I adequately understand God's love for you
whom He created to be the Mother of his Son?
God owed it to Himself to create for his only begotten Son
the most perfect Mother even He could create.
I like to believe, O Mary that God could not create
a being holier than you.
Even the highest angel was never called upon
to be so closely united with Him
through whom all things were made.
Your holiness cannot be exaggerated.
Only the holiness of Jesus is superior to your holiness.
His is infinite, yours is finite
but your holiness is a reflection of his.
It is willed by God.
Help me to understand the closeness of your relationship
with the Father and the Holy Spirit
as well as with your God—Son.
You are all holy because you are full of grace,
the most richly favoured by God of all his creatures.
Holy Mother, then look on this poor, sinful world.
Use your unique holiness to draw all your children
nearer to your Son.

O Mary, my Mother, my Queen.
God's message came to you at Nazareth
in poverty and obscurity.
God willed that He should find you
in a wretched village of no account
with no visible signs of dignity and splendour.
The advent of the Word Incarnate
is marked by simplicity.
The people of Galilee were regarded with contempt,
O Mary, by those in authority among the Jews.
Your village is never mentioned in the Old Testament.
To whom did you first relate the story
of the angel's visit?
St. Luke who was inspired to reveal it
tells us nothing of mere human interest
for that could overshadow the great central fact,
which made your consent mark the
most important moment of all time.
You were saluted by the Archangel
as "Full of Grace", the permanent recipient
of the highest favour of God.
No other creature of God, O Mary,
is more completely endowed than you with divine grace.
Your consent made you Mother of God
but also the channel of all graces received by others,
Your question to Gabriel indicated not doubt but belief.
I thank you, Mother dear, for exalting for all time
the glory of virginity assumed for love of God.
The angel assured you, O blessed Virgin,
that God's design would not affect your vow.
Your Child was to have no father but God.
Mother, obtain for me by your prayers
the grace to be always pure and innocent.
Look over me always.
Help me to shun every evil thought.
Help me to guide my eyes.
The world around me is full of temptation.
Keep me as an island in an ocean of sin,
an island endowed with the beauty of virtue.
Yes, Mother, keep me in mind and body like your Son.

85   HOLY MOTHER

How privileged I am, O Mother of God,
to be able to address you as my own Mother.
I believe that to make you his Mother
God had to make you perfect.
I cannot comprehend your holiness
I know it far surpasses the holiness of every other creature.
Your holiness grew, O Mother,
through your daily intimate life with your Son
who was and is holiness without limit.
You were always full of grace
but day by day your capacity for grace increased.
I love to call you the sanctuary of all graces.
My dearest Mother you are more beautiful than beauty,
more lovely than loveliness, more holy than holiness.
You are the only creature who has become
the dwelling place of all the graces of the Holy Spirit.
How wonderful was the perfection of your union with your Son.
Tell me about the intimacy and secrecy of your heart.
Your faith comprehended as far as any creature could
all the mysteries of salvation.
You were imbued perfectly with the spirit of Christ.
I know I cannot exalt you too much.
You shine forth for eternity as the masterpiece of God.
You have all the virtues in the highest degree
and you are the model of all of them.
Your faith, dear Mother, is the motive of your blessedness.
Your hope always grew but climaxed
as you stood beneath the cross of your Son.
Your love of God is perfect in its ardour and continuity.
Your love of all men was manifest
when you visited Elizabeth and when you
pleaded with your Son at Cana.
You united your chastity to the sufferings of your Jesus.
Your love made you the Mother of Mercy.
O Mother I believe that by your love and your prayers
you can make me grow in holiness.
Do that for me, Mother dear.
Fill me with true supernatural charity
and cause that charity to show itself
in the practice of every virtue.

O my dear Mother, talk to me
about the moment of your consent.
From all eternity it was present
in the mind of God.
He knew that his will was safe with you.
He created you to give a human body
to the Second Person of the Blessed Trinity.
To your consent we owe all that the Incarnation
has meant to earth and heaven.
To it we owe our Redemption.
If you had not freely consented
we would never have had the words and example of Jesus.
There would have been no Church.
O Mother, I cannot imagine human history without Christianity
You must know what would have happened.
I thank you now, Mother, for the Church
and for all the Church has done for our race.
I thank you for Christian civilization,
for Christian art, music, literature and architecture.
I thank you for the Saints,
for all the apostles, martyrs, doctors, confessors and holy women.
I thank you for the help of their prayers,
for their teaching
and for the inspiration and encouragement of their example.
In particular, my dear Mother,
I thank you for the conversion of my country
and for all that Christianity has meant to us.
Indeed, as I contemplate the debt of humanity
to that free consent of yours
I am overcome.
One thing follows another.
It becomes an endless litany.
O Mother, keep on mothering our world.
Irreligion, vice, immorality, cruelty and violence
seem to be producing tensions greater than ever.
Queen of Peace, Gentle Mother, Loving Virgin
intensify your prayer for us.
If that is not possible beg your Son
to raise up Saints to lead more of us to Him.

87 MARY'S PRIVILEGES

O Mother Mary, I find myself quite unable
to ponder or comprehend all you meant
to the plan of God for our sanctification and redemption.
In you were fulfilled the words of Isaiah:
"A shoot shall sprout from the stump of Jesse
and from his roots a bud shall bloom" (Isaiah 11,1)
You, Mary, are the root from which Christ
the lily of the valleys sprung.
You are the stem on which the divine Flower of salvation,
Jesus the world's Redeemer, blossomed.
For centuries our world, our race had waited for you.
Now the Church can sing of you:
"The Lord begot me, the firstborn of his ways" (Prov. 8,22)
Yes, you are the incomparably beloved daughter of the Father.
His Son is your Son.
Your free consent made you the Mother of the Word made Flesh.
So I hear Elizabeth greeting you,
"How have I deserved that the mother of my Lord should come to me?
(Luke 1, 43).
When you bowed your lovely head with consenting words on your lips
an ordination ceremony took place,
the ordination of the great High Priest of the order of Melchisedech.
You, Mother, were the sanctuary of the ordination;
a sanctuary immaculate, free from every stain,
swept pure by the gift of God,
your Immaculate Conception.
You were a sanctuary adorned with the flowers of the rarest virtues.
The assistants at the ordination ceremony were the angels of God.
They were the choir too. The ordaining prelate was the Holy Spirit,
as within you God the Son became a priest.
My priesthood and all Christian priesthood
is a sharing of the priesthood which began in you.
How can I hope to thank you?
Dear Mother, all the praises of the choirs of angels
cannot thank you as you deserve.
Every holy Mass is owed to your free consent,
every Holy Communion,
every Benediction, every absolution, every converting,
every ordination, every priestly act.

My sweet Mother, I dare to talk to you again.
I pause to listen to you talking to me.
I believe that when Gabriel saluted you
you understood that by the power of the Holy Spirit
you had conceived the Word of God.
You knew the Scriptures.
You understood them through the gift of the Holy Spirit.
You were and are his Spouse.
Your consent made you the Mother of God.
It merited for you the royal dignity of Queenship.
In my prayer now I try to enter your soul
and to understand your thoughts as you heard Gabriel say,
"He shall be called the Son of the Most High
and the Lord God shall give Him
the throne of David, his Father
and He shall reign over the house of Jacob for ever
and of his Kingdom there shall be no end" (Luke 1, 32-33)
This moment when, full of grace,
you replied to the Archangel sent to you by God
lights up your whole personality and mission.
It is the origin of all your glories.
At this moment, O Mother, I believe
that you received the royal office
of watching over the unity and peace of the human race.
Guide now the rulers of the nations,
guide the hearts of all people,
lead them from conflict to concord
and from enmity to charity.
As you consented to the request of the angel
you represented the whole of humanity
and consented to a spiritual marriage
between the Son of God and human nature.
So you made possible all that was to follow
in the life, Passion and Resurrection of Christ.
Oh, how I wish that all men
could honour you and your motherhood
and implore all your power to heal the wounds of our race.

89 THE VISITATION

When you heard from the heavenly messenger
that your relative Elizabeth was to be a mother
love surged up within you.
You set off on the journey of eighty miles to Hebron.
What thoughts were in your mind as you travelled!
They say you were still a young girl.
You carried within you
the God who made you.
Did you already adore Him?
Did you ponder about all you knew
the Scriptures had foretold about Him?
He was to be a Man of Sorrows, filled with grief.
They would pierce his hands and feet.
Did you think now, my sweet Mother,
that you were to be the Queen of Martyrs?
Thought after thought about the mystery of Salvation
must have come to you on the way.
Then you heard Elizabeth greet you.
For the first time human lips hailed you as the Mother of God.
Already you were the channel of grace.
John the Baptist leaped for joy in his mother's womb.
He was sanctified by the grace of the Divine Redeemer
So it has been ever since.
The God who called on you to
share so closely in his plan to redeem men
ordained that no grace will be granted to us
except through you.
Saint after Saint and Pope after Pope
have proclaimed that this is so.
Mary, visit me now as you visited Elizabeth.
Bring grace to me as you did to her.
Light a fire of light and love in my heart.
Let me never forget you.
Elizabeth said you were blessed
because you believed.
Pray for me that my faith will reflect yours
and that I shall trust you
as you trusted the Word of God.

Mary, I know you are with me in spirit.
I know you never cease to mother me.
Help me to ponder some of the truths about you
proclaimed by the Saints, the Pope and the Church.
Said St. Bernard, quoted by Pope Leo XIII,
"God has ordained that no grace will be granted to us
except through Mary".
And St. Alphonsus, "It is a doctrine preached by all the saints
that no grace can come to us from heaven
without passing through Mary's hands".
St. Germanus, too, "No one will be saved or obtain mercy
except through you, O heavenly Lady".
St. Louis Marie de Montfort: "To be greatly devoted to Mary
means to possess the keys to God's treasures".
St. Bernard again: "Mary, is the fertile valley
in which all the beauties of heaven are gathered".
St. Bonaventure wrote: "Remember this well:
No one will enter heaven without passing through Mary
as one would pass through a door".
Mother I believe all this.
You are so powerful before God
that to be devoted to you is a sign of predestination.
Gazing from heaven upon men
you know who is most in need of God"s grace.
You love all your children with a love we cannot fathom.
You are the tireless dispenser of divine graces.
Surely whoever loves you and lives in that love
will always enjoy a greater abundance of graces
because of his love which you will return.
Our salvation, O Mary, is in your hands.
Watch over us so that we shall always
serve your Son, our Creator, King and Redeemer
with greater and ever-growing fervour.
You went to John the Baptist as the first tabernacle of the Lord.
Pray for us so that we shall love Jesus in all his tabernacles,
in all men and in his Church.

91 MODEL OF VIRTUES

How wonderful God is to give us you, O Mary,
as an example of all virtues.
Your faith, hope and charity are perfect
because they are God's gift to you.
But how can I imitate your moral virtues?
Your purity is unsurpassed.
Help me to struggle against temptation.
Help young people to-day to overcome their passions
and the temptations of the world. Give us courage, too, Mother,
that bold will which, when faced with difficulties
and surrounded by dangers and obstacles,
is always able to make the right decisions
and to put them into practice with unconquerable energy.
May we all turn to your fortitude
and allow it to sweep away tiredness and doubt.
Mary, pray for the leaders of men in to-day's world
that they will face with courage and perseverance
the arduous problems of society.
Mother, you are the Seat of Wisdom
who penetrated beyond all belief into the
deep secrets of divine wisdom.
Mother, you are full of humility.
Willingly you are poor to be all God's.
You are faithful to God and to your own duties.
Almost all your life was filled with silence.
At Cana you gave us an example of caring foresight.
Your Magnificat proclaims your gratitude.
Mother, I see in you the purest and most faithful love
for your chaste spouse.
Your love was made up of sacrifices and of delicate attentions.
In you I find entire and continuous dedication
to needs of family and home, your spouse and your Son.
Your spiritual and corporal beauty
surpasses that of all other creatures.
Mother, your divine Son's beauty originated from you.
When the Word wished to become flesh
and to be born of a woman his love created you
the most ideally perfect of all his creatures.
Artists, poets and saints have aspired ardently
but always in vain to give your beauty adequate expression.
Mother, teach me to love you as your Son deserves.

D

Mother dear, how can anyone not be mesmerised
by the story of the birth of your Son?
I think of your journey.
I walk in spirit with you from Nazareth.
Tell me as I pause to contemplate it—
what did you and Joseph talk about on the way?
Did he know of your privileges then?
Had you explained all to him?
Had you revealed to him the prophecies of Scripture?
How did you pray together?
I accompany you as you seek for shelter.
If only those who refused had known
that their Creator was alive in you!
Did you think of the angels who were with you?
Did you wonder what it would be like
to gaze on the baby face of the God Who made you?
After God it is impossible to think of anything greater than his Mother.
Did you ponder, did you tell Joseph or did you just understand
that by choosing you, specially creating you to be his Mother
God loved you more than all the angels together.
Did your humility and your simplicity help you to realise
that your motherhood of God flooded you
with a quantity of grace
superior to all the grace in heaven?
You must have known that God had given you
everything of beauty, purity and holiness
that a creature could possibly possess.
Now, indeed, like the heavenly Father
you could call the Eternal Word your Son.
Mary you are the Mother of Him who
taught us to say "Our Father, who art in heaven".
Help me to understand the meaning and implications
of your condition as you travelled to Bethlehem.
God's human body was being completely formed in you.
You had a natural power over Him for everything.
From Him you can obtain everything you desire.
Oh, suppliant omnipotence,
entering a cattle shed to hold your Creator in your hands,
Guard me as you guarded Jesus on that journey
Form me spiritually as you formed Him physically.

93   EUCHARISTIC BETHLEHEM

Gentle, loving Mother, you see all the Masses
being celebrated at every moment of the day
somewhere in the world.
Do they make you think of Bethlehem?
The Cathedrals and churches,
great like St. Peter's in Rome,
tiny and poor like a hut in a mission field,
are poverty and simplicity when compared with the grandeur that
rightly befits the King of Kings
The candles on the altar
must remind you of St. Joseph's lantern.
The servers make you think of the angels
who must have been with you at Bethlehem.
The congregation are the modern shepherds
who have come to adore.
The altar cloth reminds you of the swaddling clothes
in which you wrapped your divine Child.
Do you see in the priest yourself
holding Christ as you once held Him?
Is not the consecrated host like his baby Body,
so small, so delicate, so pure?
Those who receive Holy Communion become like you
as they carry Jesus away within them,
Through Holy Communion the same Jesus,
who became incarnate in your womb lives in our hearts.
Pray, Mother, that all who receive Holy Communion
will be as pure of heart as you were
when your Creator came to live in you.
Mary, give me fervent devotion to Holy Mass
like that which burned in your heart at Bethlehem
Make my inner dispositions like yours
as you went to Bethlehem
and as you held Jesus in your arms.
Mother in heaven pray that I will be able
to adore, love and pray as you did
when you saw Him for the first time.
Obtain for me by your prayers
all the joy and warmth
that filled your soul at Bethlehem.

Mary, Mother dear, what did the shepherds tell you
when they came to the stable?
Did they describe the song of the angels?
Did they tell you what they saw?
Did they understand what the angel said to them?
"On earth peace to men"
You knew, Mother, about original sin.
The archangel had told you that you were full of grace
You understood how Adam's sin injured the glory of God
and brought sorrow to men.
You knew that the mystery in which you were taking part
restored God's glory
and returned peace to the world.
Because you are Immaculate, Mother dear,
you are the Queen of Peace.
You are Queen of Peace, too,
because you gave the world the Prince of Peace.
O Mary, in your heart reigned a peace
that you alone can give.
Only that peace can fill the heart.
It is the peace of an immaculate conscience,
the peace of true love,
the peace of good will,
of complete abandonment to God's will.
Your Son was to tell the world:
"Peace I leave with you, my peace I give to you" (John 14, 29).
It was your consent that brought into the world
Him who is the world's peace.
O Mother, pray that the leaders of the nations
will find peace by embracing the teaching of your Son.
Pray that all your children will become worthy of the peace of Jesus
by always seeking to please God.
Mary, pray that men will turn to you
as the Queen of Peace
as the Mediatrix of Peace
as the arbiter of peace between God and man,
as the guide and mistress of peace.
You long for peace in the world.
You are the hope of peace.
Pray that all men will understand that devotion to you
is the way to peace.

95 MARY AND PRIESTS

Mary, Mother of the Eternal High Priest,
you are in a special way Mother of all the priests of your Son.
They share in his priesthood.
At their ordination priests are called "other Christs".
That is their noblest title.
It signifies their vocation.
Mother, because there never has been any human love
to compare with your love for your Son,
so I cannot understand or comprehend
the immensity of your love for priests.
How ardently you long for them all to be worthy of their calling.
When they pronouce the words of consecration
it is your Son who comes into their hands.
You and Holy Mass are inseparable.
Your sorrows, O Mother, must have embraced your distress
at all the the Masses which are celebrated unworthily.
You cannot suffer now in glory, O Mother,
but the suffering you endured on earth
in union with the sufferings of your Son
must have included the sorrow you must feel
when priests, "other Christs", are unworthy.
How you love those whom your Son has called to his priesthood!
O Mother, summon all priests to live in you.
Form them to live as you would have them live
Pray that they will be as zealous in their apostolate
as your Son wishes them to be.
You are Mother of the Church.
Priests are at the heart of the Church
The work and life of the Church depends on priests.
God has entrusted them to your special care.
Pray that priests will be holy.
Be with them in all their thoughts and words and deeds.
Shield them against temptation.
Whisper into their minds the highest ideals.
Let them never be satisfied with mediocrity.
Be to all priests, O Mother, a source of grace and of strength.
Guide them all in every aspect of their apostolate.
Be with them at the altar, in the pulpit and in the confessional.
Pray for them all, everywhere and always.

What did the angel really say to you, Mother?
With your fullness of the Holy Spirit's gifts what did you understand?
Was it "Hail, O favoured one"?
Or was it "Hail, full of grace"?
No matter, nothing could exceed that joy of yours,
Nothing could exceed this grace granted to you alone by God.
It is impossible to imagine anything more magnificent
or more pleasing.
Nothing can come anywhere near the marvel we see in you.
All things, even the greatest of the angelic hosts
lie far below the grace, dignity and favour that are yours.
Your stateliness overshadows them all.
Well, we know, dear Mother, that nothing created
can stand in your way.
No creature of your divine Son
would not gladly acknowledge your supremacy.
Oh, if only all men could praise you
in a manner proportionate to the privileges God has given you!
You it was whom God choose
to change the condemnation of Eve into a blessing.
Because of you and through you,
Adam, who was hitherto cast down and condemned
received a blessing.
It was through your free consent
that the Father's blessing came to mankind
and reprieved them from the sentence of exclusion from heaven.
Through you those who had died before you
found God's salvation.
He who lived within you was and is
the Way, the Truth and the Life.
Through you men would follow Him who is the Way,
through you they would learn wisdom from Him who is the Truth,
through you they would receive the life
which is a sharing in God's life
and which will flower into the beatific vision.
That free consent of yours made it possible
for the supreme Creator to fill all things
with the life-giving warmth of his radiance.
Mother, how can I ever hope to thank you?
Pray that my life will be a loving song of thanks
for all you have done, do and will yet do for me.

97   MARY, OUR MOTHER

O my Mother, in holy Writ, the liturgy and the writing of the Saints
you are called God's bride, God's mother
and the best of his handmaidens.
What return can one make for all you have done for us?
Is any gift that it is my power to give adequate for you?
I owe you honour, I owe you devotion,
I owe you love, I owe you praise.
The honour I owe you is far more than I can give
for you are the Mother of my infinite Lord.
When I honour you I honour Him.
Because you are his Mother
you are my Mother, too.
You are the channel of divine life to me.
If you had not graciously consented to become God's mother
I would still be in darkness.
I would have received none of the fruits of the Cross.
The Church and the Sacraments came from the
wounded side of your Son.
Without your free consent it would never have happened.
Yes, Mother, speak to me now.
Give me faith to understand
all that baptism means to me and to all Christians.
Through baptism corruption was banished for incorruption.
Sin was replaced by innocence.
Death gave way to life.
From baptism came wisdom, righteousness,
sanctification, redemption.
Sweet Mary, you are mother of them all.
I owe them all to you.
In return all I can offer is myself
by complete consecration of all that I am, all that I have.
Accept my consecration as an act of homage.
In you I praise God and his holy works.
In you He fashioned Himself
who is wonderful beyond all wonder.
You have given Him to me
in the Church and in the Sacraments.
The life of my soul is his life.
Mother, raise up many more of your children
to appreciate and understand these truths
by the gift of the Holy Spirit whose Spouse you are.

In saying this, O Mother, you were praising God
for all the extraordinary, unique and special gifts
you received from Him.
You give yourself wholly to God.
You were dedicated to giving all your spiritual energies
to God's praise and service.
Pray, Mother, that I may never stray from my dedication
to the loving service of your Son.
Give me the mind which will find its main delight
in contemplating the infinite attributes of God.
How you must have delighted to ponder on those infinite perfections.
As you visited Elizabeth you knew that you carried within you
the infinitely perfect Creator.
How you just have looked forward to seeing Him!
What a thrill the greeting of Elizabeth must have given you!
O Mother, I admire your spirit of truth and humility.
"He who is mighty has done great things for me" you say.
You attribute nothing to your own merits
but everything to Him.
He who has made you so uniquely holy
is power, holiness and greatness Himself.
May I, Mother, by your prayers
practice a humility like yours.
You remind all who read or hear your canticle to think of the limitless
holiness of God.
"Holy is his Name".
That is the name holier than all others
You invite all to call on it
and to take refuge in it.
It is by calling on that divine name
that man will find his salvation.
You remind us, too, of the infinite mercy of God,
of how his limitless love bends down to us in our weakness.
O Mary, pray that I shall never fail
to call on the benevolence, the clemency and the compassion
of Him who for our sake
did such wonderful things to you.
Obtain for me the gift of understanding
so that whenever I recite your "Magnificat"
nothing of its wisdom shall escape me.

99   JESUS TOOK A MYSTICAL BODY

Mary, mother me, teach me, guide me,
Fill me with your faith and your understanding.
Jesus took mortal flesh in your womb.
But He took also a mystical Body.
We are that Body.
We were born of you with Him.
Mother, I believe with all my heart
that you are really my mother
because you have given me the life of my soul.
Your heart is the heart of a mother which
poured forth on us the fullness of love.
Your immense love for us, O Mother,
so overcame you that
in order to have us as your children
you freely offered your beloved Jesus
to divine Justice for our salvation.
You stood beneath the Cross on Calvary
not as if stunned by the terrible sight
but as if you were happy to sacrifice your Son for us.
There was only one sacrifice on Calvary, Mother dear.
You and your Son offered the same holocaust
with the same heart full of love.
Mother, I ponder how years and years
before I was born I was already living in your Heart.
You had already loved me and suffered for me.
Mother, I do not want to think of you
as if you were my mother.
I believe that you are really my Mother.
You are bound to me by mysterious bonds.
Even in the natural order bonds exist, tightly tied
Which join the life of a mother to the life of her child.
In the spiritual, supernatural order
those bonds are stronger in much the same way
as the conclusions of faith are firmer than the conclusions of reason.
Mother, I love you, warmly, deeply, most sincerely.
I can give you so little.
It is you who are the most generous one,
You give me so much for so little.
Give me deep, beautiful, holy, fruitful piety.

Mother Mary, I know that being united with you
means being united with your divine Son.
When from all eternity God conceived you
and destined you to be his mother
He willed to make you as perfect as ever He could.
You are the only being whom God created
precisely to show what a perfect being He could make.
You are the spotless mirror of the majesty of God.
You alone, among creatures, are the perfect picture of God,
absolutely perfect, free from all defects
endowed with every gift, natural and supernatural
in the highest degree in which God has ever willed
that they should be found in a pure creature.
As I gaze on you in my prayer
I understand that you have attained the peak of perfection
that God has decreed his creatures could realise.
You give to Him the maximum glory
He wishes to derive from creation.
Because He made you to be his Mother
God surely willed that you alone
among all creatures should display
his love, his wisdom, his goodness and his power.
In creating you God exhausted his ordinary omnipotence
He could have made a greater heaven or a greater earth,
a more brilliant sun or more numerous stars
but never a greater Mother.
Such is your perfection, my own dear Mother,
that nothing beyond it is conceivable under God.
None can ever comprehend it but God.
How proud I am to know that in you, my Blessed Virgin Mother,
all that pertains to perfection must be found.
Mother Church applies to you these inspired words of wisdom.
"For she is a vapour of the power of God
and a certain pure emanation of the glory of Almighty God . . .
She is more beautiful than the sun
and above all the order of the stars
being compared with light she is always found before it"
(Wisdom 7,29).
How wonderful it is for me to know and believe as I do
that you are indeed the Mother God has given me.

101   FULL OF GRACE

God, my loving Father, you gave Moses detailed plans
for the construction of the Ark of the Covenant.
Precious metals were to be used.
The work was executed with scrupulous attention.
It was handled with awe and reverence.
It was the centre and heart of the Jewish people.
It contained your word, O God, written on stone
And the Manna rained down from heaven.
Your glory appeared over it from time to time.
When God the Son became man
You gave us another Ark;
an immaculate vessel fitted out and perfectly adorned.
This Ark was to contain not merely your passing word
written on stone
but your everlasting substantial Word made flesh.
It was to contain not the Manna
but the true life-giving bread from heaven.
The new Ark you have given us
did not merely contain the Word made flesh.
She was your own mother, one flesh and blood with You.
O God, You planned the living Ark of the New Covenant,
your blessed Mother from eternity,
Designed by your infinite wisdom
she was created by your almighty work,
Father, Son and Holy Spirit.
Mother, now I turn to you.
Teach me to thank God for You.
On you the Holy Spirit came down.
You the power of the Most High overshadowed. What an exquisite
tabernacle you are,
a precious monstrance made by God Himself.
Your body is the gem of God's creation.
It is the wonder of the angels.
The holiness of your soul, ever full of grace,
surpassed the accumulated sanctity of all the angels and saints.
My loving Mother, I think of you now
as completely taken up in God and filled by Him,
as clothed with the divine Sun.
Mother, look on me, love me,
I am overcome by the vision of your holiness.

O Mary, loving Mother, I turn to you in prayer.
Help me to understand the greeting you heard from the angel.
"Hail, full of grace"—solemn and unparalleled.
A salutation never heard before.
You were, and still are, the seat of all divine graces.
Living in such intimate contact with your God-Son
your capacity for grace must have grown by the minute.
But it was always full,
always adorned with all the gifts and fruits of the Holy Spirit.
Your gifts and graces surpassed the accumulated perfection
of all the angels and saints put together.
Mother, how immense is the total of all the graces
conferred on the angelic hosts and the saints.
But, Mother, tell me; guide me,
Am I not right in believing that if we add them all up
they will not equal your grace?
Mother Church applies to you the inspired words.
"In me is all the grace of the way and the truth,
in me is all hope of life and strength" (Sir. 24,25).
O Mother, I love to honour you.
God has given you to me to be my very own mother.
As I gaze on you in my mind I see in you
the purity of the angels and the faith of the Patriarchs.
I see the knowledge of the Prophets and the zeal of the Apostles.
I see the patience of the Martyrs
and the devotedness of the Confessors.
I see the innocence of the Virgins and the simplicity of children.
I know, dear Mother, that God could not deny you
any gift He made to angels and saints.
The power and the wisdom of God are in you.
Within your womb lived God Himself in created grace.
After He was born, the holy Trinity dwelt in you
in as complete a way as possible.
Your fullness of grace never ceased to grow.
How beautiful are the words applied to you Mother, by a Saint
"She was the dawn at her birth, the day at the birth of Christ,
the sun itself at her death".
Yes, dear Mother, I see you as a flash of living lightning
rising to the summits of the Eternal Hills
and burying itself in the inaccessible light
of the everlasting Trinity.

103 MOTHER OF GOD

How wonderful, indescribably marvellous it is
to know that you, God's mother are my mother too
The foundation, the sum total, the crown of all your graces and
privileges, dear Mother, is your divine Motherhood.
No creature can understand your sublime, immense graces.
Even though I had a million tongues
I could never express your greatness.
It belongs not merely to the supernatural order but to the divine.
Tell me, Mother, am I not right in believing
that your dignity is an a sense infinite
because it derives from the infinite good that is God?
When you conceived and gave birth to God
you hovered on the confines of the Divinity.
Surely such divinely unique dignity
must be surrounded by every possible grace and privilege.
Creatures, dear Mother, receive life and being from God.
But you on their behalf gave a creaturely life and being to God.
Through you, Mary, God gave man his Divinity
and man gives God his humanity.
What an admirable transaction!
Oh, why do not all Christian people see
that you are the link of this indescribable, unutterable transaction
You occupy in the whole universe a middle place
between the creature and the Incarnate God.
I pray now with St. Anselm. I believe that
"all nature is created by God, and God is born of you, Mary.
God brought about all things
and through you, Mother, He created Himself.
Thus he re-created all He had created.
He who could make all things from nothing
would not remake them without you.
God is the Father of all created things.
You Mary, are Mother of all re-created things.
God is the Father in the constitution, the creation, of all things.
You, Mary, are mother in the restitution, the restoration of all things.
God begot Him without whom nothing at all exists.
You, Mary, brought forth Him without whom nothing is well at all".
You clothed your God with the flesh,
He has clothed you with the glory of his majesty.
O inexpressible wonder of wonders.

My dear Mother Mary, I want to pray about Cana.
I want to think with you about what happened at the wedding feast.
With your motherly care you saw
how the young couple were sure to be embarrassed.
You look now on all your children in the same way.
You know our every need.
You pray to your Son for us,
"They have no wine".
For 'Wine', Mother I can substitute any virtue.
Your Son called you 'Woman'.
You and He must have discussed together the story of Genesis.
You knew that you were the woman
in that first prophecy of Redemption.
So now, when your Jesus, calls you 'Woman'
you understand the deeper inner meaning of it.
You are indeed, preeminently, THE WOMAN.
You, Mother, understood His reply.
As soon as you heard it you asked the attendants
to prepare for a miracle.
Jesus was not rebuking you.
There was no fuss, no embarrassment, no scene
about your coming request.
Had He a gentle smile on his lips
and a kindly look in his eye as he replied to you?
"My time has not yet come"
Mother, surely these words tell us something stupendous,
that a miracle was worked entirely because you asked for it.
Am I right in seeing here an indication, if I dare suggest such a thing,
that God will go out of his way to fulfill your wishes?
But you could not ask for anything against his will, could you?
Saints have seen you here commanding God with motherly authority.
So I pray now and always
"Show yourself a Mother".
This very title seems to give you a right and authority
over the Lord of the world.
"Whatsoever He shall say to you, do it".
Thank you, Mother, for giving us such a formula for living.
When the attendants at Cana acted on it a miracle followed.
Obtain for me the grace to act on it too
so that my poor efforts at virtue will be turned into
the wine of real holiness.

105   FOUND IN THE TEMPLE

The story of the loss and finding of your divine Son, Mary,
is full of profound mystery.
The union between you and Jesus is close and indissoluble.
You were in no way to blame for losing Him.
He could commit no fault in remaining in the Temple.
When you found Him He spoke his first recorded word.
It must have been with a smile in his eyes
and in a tone of gentle affection.
Did you only come to realise the deeper meaning of his words
when you pondered them in your heart?
Or was the ultimate significance unveiled to you
after your Son's Resurrection?
When He spoke to you as you found Him
did His words conceal the assertion
that ultimately He was called by his heavenly Father to Jerusalem
to accomplish there the salvation of the world?
So in this one sentence of your twelve year old Son
ia concentrated all his future destiny.
Even with the fullness of your faith its complete truth
could not be clear until his glorious Resurrection.
Am I right, dear Mother, in concluding
that what St. Luke says you did not understand was
that in those first recorded words
your Jesus was darkly alluding to
his future Passion and Resurrection in the Holy City?
You told Him that Joseph and you had looked for Him sorrowing.
What motherly love was in those words to Jesus.
They could not be a reproach because Jesus was perfection itself,
and you were not ignorant of his dignity and mission.
Your words were no more than a simple question
in the natural language of a loving Mother.
Your sorrow at losing Jesus was not like any other sorrow.
You loved Him more purely than any other mother loved her son.
You knew He could not do wrong
nor hurt you without love.
Your conversation together when you had found Him
must have been full of tenderest love,
quiet and intimate and full of divine understanding.
Mother, help me all through my life to search for your Jesus.

SORROWING MOTHER

My dearest loving Mother, the sufferings of your Son
must have been before you all your life.
As you pondered the Scriptures in the Temple,
enlightened by the Holy Spirit's gifts of wisdom and understanding
you must have known how his earthly life would end.
In the quiet days in Nazareth did you talk together
about all that lay ahead?
Your sufferings are unique.
Help me to see them in the context of your
intimate union with your Son.
No other man or woman could suffer like you
because no other person was so closely united with
the suffering Saviour.
By the special design of the loving Providence of God
you were near Jesus on his way to death
and at the foot of his Cross.
His Passion and Death were in a sense
your passion and death too
because you utterly surrendered your motherly rights over Jesus.
You comprehended, as far as a creature could comprehend,
the Eternal Father's love for men.
It was so great that in order to save us
He willed the death of his Son, your Son.
You understood as no other the infinite love of your Son
in wishing to die for us.
You understood how perfectly He willed to conform Himself
to the will of the Father.
You, too, dear Mother, intimately united with the Holy Trinity
with your entire will
offered and consented to your Son's suffering and death,
so that we might be saved.
What does our race owe to Jesus for his Passion?
What do we owe to you, suffering Mother, for your compassion?
You suffered bitterly but you rejoiced greatly at the same time
because a sacrifice was offered for the Redemption of all.
Only by the ocean of grace you received through your Son's death
was your Immaculate Heart ever able to support this infinite sorrow.
The Passion of your divine Son was mirrored
in every detail in your loving Heart.
Mother, through your sorrow help me to understand all sorrow.

107 QUEEN OF MARTYRS

Mary, my loving Mother, into your pure Heart
your intense love of your divine Jesus
drew all his pains and torments,
all his suffering and sorrows
his wounds, every detail of his Passion
and even his death.
The same nails which crucified Him
crucified also your Immaculate Heart;
so close and intimate was your loving union with Him.
The thorns which you saw piercing his head
pierced also your perfect soul.
Through your condolence and compassion
you had the same sorrows that your Son suffered,
the same Passion, the same sword of death.
Your Heart, gentle Mother, was one with your Son
in a union so perfect that
nothing could wound Him without wounding you.
When your motherly breast was wounded by love
you were far from seeking a cure of your wound.
Instead, you loved it more than any healing.
You cherished the marks of sorrow
that love engraved in your Heart.
You desired continually to die of this wound
since your Son died of it
amid the flames of charity,
a perfect holocaust for all the sins of the world.
Other martyrs sacrificed their own lives
but you, O Blessed Virgin, consummated your martyrdom
by sacrificing the life of your Son,
a life which you loved far more than your own.
That sacrifice meant for you pain
which exceeded all other torments ever endured on earth.
As the sun surpasses all the stars in lustre
so your sorrows my dear Mother surpass
all the tortures of the martyrs.
You were a martyr not by the executioner's sword
but by the bitter sorrow of your Heart.
Mother, I offer all the suffering of my life
in union with the sufferings you had to bear.

O Mary, loving, humble Mother,
you proclaimed that great things had been done to you
by Him who is mighty.
You believe that the power to produce grace
belongs to God alone.
But humility is truth,.
You must have known that the intimacy of your union with Christ
and your association with Him in the work of Redemption
were the reasons why you merited by fitness
all that your Jesus merited by justice.
How often must I proclaim the truth
to make its meaning live in my soul!
How often have Saints and Popes called you
the Almoner of God's graces,
the Dispensatrix, the Mediatrix.
the Treasurer of the divine Mercies,
the Advocate of the whole world,
the living Storehouse of all good things.
I believe, dear Mother, that God has entrusted you
with the keeping, the administration and the distribution of
all His graces.
All of them pass through your hands and
according to the power you have received over them
you give to whom you will, the way you will,
when you will and as much as you will
the graces of the eternal Father,
the virtues of Jesus Christ
and the gifts of the Holy Spirit.
Mother, I want to love you as you deserve to be loved.
I want to surrender myself to you, all that I am, all that I have.
This is what you deserve.
I know that by trying to live this consecration
I become an instrument of your immense power.
Give me your strength, your magnetism
to come ever nearer to you and to your Son
and by so doing to bring with me a legion of souls
who will love you more and spread around them faith in you,
hope in you and trust in you
to the mighty degree that you deserve.

109   QUEEN

To-day I think of you Mother dear, as Queen.
You are indeed the Queen of Heaven,
Sovereign of the Church militant, suffering and triumphant,
Queen of Heaven, of the choirs of angels, of all the Saints.
You reign with Christ and for Christ
You partake in Christ's empire.
You reign for Him, side by side with Him,
for the grace and love of God.
Yours is above all a Queenship of excellence
You are Queen because you were born from a Kingly race,
because you are the Mother of God,
because you are Mother of Christ the King,
because you are the associated companion of Christ the King
because you are the second Eve of the second Adam.
You are Queen by title of conquest, as Co-Redemptrix.
By your sorrow you are Queen of Martyrs.
Your Queenship is not in the order of temporal queenship.
It is expressed in the heights of Heaven
not as will of dominion but as the total giving of yourself.
Your Queenship, Mary, is a co-rulership with Christ.
At the same time you are both Mother and minister of the King.
How can words describe your power, Mother and Queen.
It is superior to the power of all other creatures.
You exercise it with your Son and on Him.
Because of your intimate union with Him
God communicates to you almost all his power.
Yours is a saving power, irresistible, clement and maternal.
I praise you because you are triumphant and victorious with Christ.
You have overcome heresy, sin and the devil
Well do I know that the marvels of heaven can be represented only
through the ever imperfect words and expressions of human language.
but this does not limit the extent to which we honour you.
Your Queenship is a supernal reality.
It penetrates our innermost hearts.
It touches all that is spiritual and immortal in their very essence.
O Queen of Heaven, watch over human society,
watch over its unity and peace,
open the path of faith to the world.
I offer you now all my faith, my submission,
my service and my love.

O my Blessed Mother, the birth of your Son
was like the penetration of glass by light.
It was like the coming forth of his glorified Body
from his sealed tomb.
It was like his coming into the Cenacle through closed doors.
Why do we try to reason about your holy virginity?
Why do we so unnecessarily tire our minds?
Why should the way of divine Majesty surprise us?
Why must we express surprise at the wonderful ways of God?
I ponder quietly now a multiple mystery.
You, Mary, a creature became the Mother of your Creator.
You, a virgin, became a mother that remained ever a virgin.
The meeting of extremes was the greatest miracle of all;
the paradox of a God becoming a creature
without ceasing to be God.
The next I see as the counterpart of the first—
you, Mary, a Virgin becoming God's Mother
without ceasing to be a Virgin.
God Himself singled out your miraculous virginity
as the stupendous sign with which
to convert an unbelieving race.
Isaiah said it, "The Lord Himself shall give you a sign.
Behold, a Virgin shall conceive and bear a Son
and his name shall be called Emmanuel" (Isaiah 7,14).
O most holy Handmaid and Mother of the Word,
Your child-birth proves you to be a Virgin
and your Virginity demonstrates you to be a Mother.
Did not the infinite dignity of the Incarnate Word
demand that his generation in time from a human mother
resemble in some way his eternal origin
from the bosom of God the Father?
Was it not unbecoming that the Son of the Heavenly Father
should have an earthly father as well?
Your Jesus, Mary, was, we proclaim, Light from the Light.
In his temporal origin He is Light from the Star.
As the star sends forth its rays without impairing itself so, without
losing your integrity, you, blessed Virgin, brought forth the Son.
As the rays do not diminish the brightness of the star
as the Son did not diminish your integrity as the Blessed Virgin.
O, Virgin Mother, pray for the purity of girls and women to-day.

When Elizabeth heard your greeting, sweetest Mother,
the babe leaped for joy in her womb.
The Precursor was cleansed of original sin.
You were already fulfilling your vocation
as the Channel of all Graces.
Elizabeth was filled with the Holy Spirit.
and cried, not quietly or gently, but with a loud voice,
"Blessed are you among women
and blessed is the fruit of your womb".
The Holy Spirit of God inspired this act of faith.
You are his Spouse.
But Elizabeth honoured you still more.
"How have I deserved that the Mother of my Lord
should come to me"?
Oh, why do not all followers of your Son
cry out as Elizabeth did, hailing and honouring you
as the Mother of God?
How great was the power of your words.
No sooner had you pronounced them
than the Holy Spirit was given.
It was by divine inspiration that Elizabeth spoke
of things past, present and future.
She knew, Mary, your infinite dignity
and your present and future glory.
In sheer wonder and ecstatic delight
she hailed you as what you are,
"Blessed among women".
You responded with the greatest, the most sublime and exalted
of all Canticles, full of mysteries
so great and hidden, that even the angels did not know them.
Saintly writers believe, blessed Mother,
that you often repeated your Magnificat to yourself
especially after Holy Communion,
and that devils tremble and flee when they hear your words,
"He has shown might in His arm.
He has scattered the proud in the conceit of their heart".
Mother, never cease to be a channel of grace to me.
Fill me with a burning desire to be like your Son.
Shield me against temptation,
Transfer to me, implant in my soul
something of your vision, your humility and your love.

Holy Spirit of God, fill my soul with Wisdom.
I know it is your gift.
let it not lie dormant, unused.
You inspired the Sacred Writers to proclaim that
Wisdom is better then gold (Prov. 16, 16).
Give me it in such generous abundance
that i am able to consider the eternal truths
and to judge all things by them.
Let them be the light of my mind.
May I always set a right value on eternal salvation.
Around me, Spirit of God, I see multitudes
who seem to have no interest in salvation.
They live as if there is no eternal reward for good,
no eternal punishment for evil.
Give me the courage to instruct as many of them as I can
as effectively as I can in the doctrine of salvation.
May I always relish the things of God.
"Fear of the Lord is the beginning of Wisdom" (Prov. 1,7).
Holy Spirit, breath into the people of the whole world
a spirit of reverence for their Creator.
With your gift of wisdom
illuminate the minds of all those who are regarded as thinkers
so that they will guide others correctly.
Illuminate indeed the minds of all people
that they may no longer walk so aimlessly as in darkness.
Moderate passions, rectify affections, direct wills.
Holy Spirit, renew the life of my soul with vigour and energy.
Draw me ever closer to more perfect union with God.
Give me facility in well-doing.
Increase my holy contempt for the riches of the earth.
Let me see all in the light of eternity.
"Wisdom does more for a person", the Wise Man says,
"than ten rulers can do for a city" (Eccles. 7,20).
Yes, Holy Spirit, through your gift of Wisdom
make me strong, give me lasting peace of mind,
endow me with stability.
Make me wise enough to pray more to be wise
not with the wisdom of this earth
but with the wisdom of God.

113 UNDERSTANDING

How I long, Holy Spirit, for your gift of understanding.
I read the lives of the Saints,
often men and women of immense simplicity.
whom the world would despise as unlettered.
Yet how they were able to penetrate the hidden meaning
of revealed truth, of mysteries.
Understanding, your gift, O Holy Spirit,
is not the natural gift of intellect or reason.
I so desire it because it deepens my spiritual vision.
It is like a lens to my spiritual eye.
It will help me so to fathom holy truth
that I will be able to live by it.
Holy Spirit. divine truth is so infinitely precious
that I want to appreciate it,
to comprehend it as well as I can,
to fathom and measure it to the inner depths.
Only then will I discern the beauty of truth
and use it to guide me in the way to perfection
and to union with the Eternal Trinity.
I beg You, Holy Spirit, by your gift
to perfect my faith
in a manner beyond the power of reason.
Elevate my mind to act above its human mode.
Enable me to penetrate the meaning of revealed truth
more profoundly than is possible by faith alone.
Give me the intensity of simple intuition.
Permit me to see all things through lively faith.
I pray, Lord, to see the substance beneath the accidents,
the meaning beneath the words,
the mysterious significance of sensible signs,
the spiritual realities contained beneath the outward appearances.
May I be like the disciples on the way to Emmaus
seeing the truths of faith in so full a light
that I am more firmly strengthened in my belief.
Holy Spirit, enable me by this precious gift
to draw from revealed principles
the theological conclusions contained in them.
Reveal to me, Lord, the things you hide
from the worldly wise and prudent.

114   KNOWLEDGE

Holy Spirit, enlighten my faith
by your gift of Knowledge.
May I always see created things in their relation to You, O God.
You manifest Yourself in all external things.
As I gaze upon all the wonders of nature
in the heavens and on the earth
illuminate my vision to see you, O God in all.
Let me see everything like a sacrament,
a visible sign of your infinite perfections.
Let me adore in spirit what your creatures represent.
Inspire me, Holy Spirit, to marvel at
the Majesty of God wherever it appears.
In a word Lord, endow me as richly as you can
with the science of the Saints.
Give me your intuition to discover in each creature
without the aid of my senses and
without the aid of my reason
the dependence of each creature upon You.
I believe, Holy Spirit, that by your gift
I acquire this knowledge instantly and without labour.
So fill me with your gift
that at a glance I shall discern the cause of all things
and in each of these find
food for prayer
and for perpetual contemplation.
May I see all created things as leading me to You, O God.
May I always remember that everything comes from your hands,
O divine Creator and Preserver.
In everything I see your likeness and reflection.
Holy Spirit, may I be able by your gift of knowledge
understand how the end and purpose of everything
is to lead me to the Creator.
Your gift enables me to feel from the rocks and cliffs,
their immovable firmness and strength,
that you, Lord, are strong and to be trusted.
The birds with their songs, the flowers with their beauty,
the ocean waves with their strength,
all lead me to joy in You, their infinite Creator
and to thank You for always, without ceasing.

115   COUNSEL

Spirit of God, endow me with your gift of Counsel,
to perfect my prudence, enabling me
always to judge promptly and rightly.
Give me an intuition
that is more supernatural than natural
to decide what must be done
especially when decisions are difficult to make.
Holy Spirit, be always with me.
When i need your Counsel, speak into my heart
to make me understand in an instant
what I must do.
Help me to counsel others with heavenly wisdom.
Be with me when I try to help others.
May I never fail to discern the means,
May I always see the way.
May I enjoy assurance
when the ways are steep, deserted or forbidding.
May I be patient enough
to wait for the acceptable time.
Show me how to reconcile interior holiness with apostolic zeal,
sincere affection for others with perfect chastity,
the simplicity of the dove with the prudence of the serpent.
May I exercise authority when such is my duty
without losing the confidence and affection
of those I wish to help.
Holy Spirit, be with me always,
ever guiding be to combine tact with rectitude and kindliness.
Enlighten me to see myself as I really am.
Show me my defects.
Counsel me to rectify them.
Convince me of my weakness.
Show me your ways, teach me your paths.
May I be always ready and able to listen to your voice
and to follow your inspirations.
Keep me, Holy Spirit, always open and docile.
Never allow me to fail to call on your help.
Permit me to look into the divine mind,
infinite mirror of light,
to discover what to do in every circumstance,
and thus enjoy peace, security and tranquillity.

Holy Spirit, I cannot tell you
how sincerely I desire your gift of fortitude
to give to my will an impulse and an energy
to do really great things for God
joyfully and fearlessly, despite all obstacles.
Take hold of my soul;
give it strong dominion over all my lower faculties
and over all difficulties from outside as well.
Give me holy determination,
fill me with assurance and joy
and the certain hope of success.
Grant that without hesitation or fear
I will do things which are most arduous.
In the midst of all my activity may I by your gift
practice perfect perfect recollection.
When i am praised or honoured
may I remain sincerely humble.
May I, even now, be ready to work for souls
in spite of tiredness or even danger or criticism.
May I always be ready to shun human respect
and to fear nothing more than sin.
I want to spend myself entirely for God's work.
Holy Spirit, make me brave enough to do it.
Make me so generous that I will never shirk any good thing
which will lead me or others to you.
Never let me forget my genuine weakness.
Rather, remembering it, may I turn to you
who alone am able to make me spiritually strong.
By your gift may I share in the very power of Christ.
Never allow me to abandon the right way because it is hard.
Spirit of love, you know my desire to be holy.
Your gift of fortitude clothes me with the strength of God.
I believe that with this gift I can conquer every difficulty.
Even the obstacles which lie in my way
become means to good in the climate of your gift.
Elevate me, Divine Spirit, above every created good
so that, conquering myself,
I will be in the heart of God
where reign boundless confidence and unchanging peace.
Endow me with courage far beyond every human courage.

117   **PIETY**

Holy Spirit, fill me with your precious gift of piety.
Perfect in me my desire to grow in spiritual childhood.
Make my devotion tender and loving.
Give me a vivid and compelling vision of God as my loving Father.
Take away from my spiritual exercises a sense of arduousness
and replace it by eagerness, devotedness, fervour and enthusiasm.
Make my love generous and tender,
always eager to do what pleases You, O God,
affectionate, lovingly abandoned to the divine Will.
Make me ever conscious of your tender mercy.
Pour your light, Spirit of God, into my soul,
touch my heart,
reveal to me ever more of the world of holiness and grace
so that I shall love You more and more.
Lead me with your holy movements.
Guide me into the world of light and love,
of generosity and elevation.
Open my mind more to your inspirations
Breathe into me, breath of God,
deeper intuition of the divinity and wonder of the life of the spirit.
Accomplish wonders in my poor unworthy heart
Lead me to discover the full meaning of the divine Fatherhood.
Give me all the eagerness and confidence of a little child.
Make me genuinely simple and sincere,
straightforward and uncomplicated.
Lead me to love as a child the Blessed Virgin
and to refer to her some of the veneration,
some of my love for God whose perfections she reflects.
As a child I wish to revere and love the angels and the Saints,
to regard Holy Writ as being a love-letter from my heavenly Father,
which tells me of his thoughts and his desires for me.
Fill me, Holy Spirit, with tender love for holy Church,
the Bride of Christ, born of his Sacred Heart,
perpetuating his mission on earth
and invested with his own infallible authority.
Inspire me to be concerned as a loving child
in whatever concerns the Church, my loving Mother,
her successes, her interests, her struggles, her joys, her sorrows.
Give me childlike veneration and love for Christ's vicar on earth.
In a word, Holy Spirit,
galvanise me to see and love God always and everywhere.

Lord God, may I never be separated from You.
Holy Spirit, inspire me with your gift of filial fear.
Kindle within me this one fear above all fears,
the fear of being separated from the God I love.
Activate in me the holy fear which is the beginning of wisdom.
Convince me that in order to possess divine Wisdom
I must be united so closely to You, O God,
that nothing can separate me from You.
Inspire me, divine Spirit, with all the profound respect
I ought to have for You, who are holiness without limit.
May I never fail in the slightest degree
to display and practice perfect respect and reverence
for the limitless perfections which are yours.
Living in this reverential awe
may I be detached from the things of this earth.
Holy Spirit, stimulate in me such holy reverence
that it will compel me to cling to all that is divine
and thus avoid all that can separate me from You.
Let me never be unduly fascinated by exterior things.
Rather may I gaze on all that reflects your infinite attributes.
May I lift my eyes to high places,
elevate my heart and mind to heaven
to penetrate into your infinite bosom, O God.
I long to contemplate You, the ineffable, infinite personal Love
which will unite me in a loving embrace
with the Father and the Son.
Holy Spirit, strengthen me so that I meditate frequently
even continuously on the infinite grandeur of God,
his attributes, his perfections, his very infinity.
Enable me, too, to understand the true nature of sin,
always an offence against infinite Majesty.
I long, Holy Spirit, for a sweet intimacy,
a loving familiarity with my heavenly Father.
May I contemplate until they become living realities for me
the divine love that brought me out of nothing,
the constant kindliness that cares for me always
and the surpassing beauty that should magnetise me.
May I never lose, but rather ever grow
in a vivid sense of your greatness O infinite God.

119   GOD PRESENT

I raise my eyes to gaze at the disc in the monstrance.
With all my heart I believe that you, Jesus are present there
with your Body, your Blood, your Soul and your Godhead,
really, truly and substantially.
You are the infinite God,
the Second Person of the Holy Trinity.
You never began to exist.
You were there for a timeless eternity before creation began.
In the fullness of time You took your human Body
from Mary's flesh and blood.
As she gazed on You when she first saw You at Bethlehem
so I gaze on You now.
In deepest faith she adored You, her infinite Creator.
With as fervent faith as I can muster I adore You too.
I try to contemplate all your divine attributes.
You are infinite perfection.
Lord, help me to understand what this means.
You are not only loving, but Love itself,
not only good, but Goodness itself,
not only wise, but Wisdom itself.
So I could name all your attributes,
each of them equal to your measureless divine Being,
absolute, boundless, fathomless, illimitable.
How can I hope to adore You as You deserve, O Sacred Host?
Nothing so stupendous exists in this world,
Words fail me as I try to tell You
all that I feel so intensely with my whole being.
Behind the whiteness of that disc You are there,
O Godhead hidden.
I think of all the treasures in the whole world,
all that are contained in galleries and museums,
I contemplate the indescribable combined beauty of all the flowers,
I am at a loss to think of the wonders of nature
that compel astonished admiration.
Then I know and believe with all my heart
that here, alone in this church, are You,
the immense, immeasurable, incomprehensible,
infinitely wise and powerful Creator of all.
O Sacred Host, I am speechless.
I wish to prostrate myself, to give you my all.

How infinitely, indescribably wonderful
is your presence, O Lord, in the Sacred Host.
What I see looks just like a white disc.
I feel it, smooth and so very ordinary
I taste it and experience the flavour of bread
Yet, You Lord, Truth itself, have said
"This is my Body".
Never once in my life have I doubted that.
I thank You for the gift of faith.
"Than Truth's own word there is no truer token".
Those standing beneath the cross to which You were nailed
saw your human Body, poor, weak, suffering.
But your Godhead remained so hidden.
Now, even your Body is concealed too.
I believe, Lord; help my unbelief.
I bow down in wonder before your humility.
Immeasurable greatness hidden under the semblance
of the commonest of foods.
Your human Body is here, Jesus,
glorified but still bearing the wounds of your Passion,
wounds you endured for love of me.
Yes, Lord, you died for me.
You continue to offer Yourself for me.
Through your dying I am able to live.
But You also give me Yourself to feed my soul.
I believe that when I was baptised
I was born again.
I received a wonderful new life,
a sharing in the life of the Divine Trinity,
a life that is indeed divine.
You, Lord, in your wonderful providence
feed everything according to its nature.
You feed the divine life of my soul
with divine food, your own very Self.
O mystery of mysteries, O mystery of faith.
I need your own gift to begin to understand it all.
How I long to cry out to the whole wide world,
"Why are you starving? Why do you refuse the food that is God"?
Lord, I do believe.
Increase my faith. Move me to share it.

121 EUCHARISTIC LORD, LIVING CORNER-STONE OF THE CHURCH

Lord Jesus, here you are in the midst of your Pilgrim-Militant Church.
How wonderfully You multiply your presence and your activities.
In every consecrated Host are all the infinite attributes of God;
limitless power is there,
indescribable love,
infinite wisdom.
Lord, give me faith simple enough to believe it all.
Holy Spirit, give me understanding to appreciate
what all this means to the Church.
There is nothing like it on earth—
all the infinite attributes of God
present in a unique way
in every tabernacle. in every consecrated Host.
Can such a wonder, O Lord, be expressed in words?
Is it because it is so imponderable that it is not appreciated?
My God, holiness is scorned in our world.
Yet your Eucharistic presence and sacrifice
is the fount of all holiness.
They make your Church the pillar and ground of truth.
They are the source of the power of the Church.
Why then, Lord, does the Church seem to be so powerless?
Why is the world still so pagan?
Why are souls not converted in their thousands?
Is it because the members of your Church
fail to comprehend, esteem and prize
the full significance of your divine presence?
What ignorance, what indifference, what apathy
dominates our world.
Little wonder that You appeal to your Saints for reparation.
King of kings, Lord of lords, God from God,
You are infinite in majesty and power
and yet so accessible.
Not only am I able to kneel here before You,
I can receive You into my very being.
Why is your Eucharistic power in the Church suppressed?
King of Ages, immortal, invisible,
use your infinite power to take away tepidity.
Release it so that the men of the world will see it
and come to learn that your sacramental presence
endows your Church with power beyond understanding.

O my Lord Jesus, You never cease
to teach me by your example in the Holy Eucharist.
What love You show, giving Yourself so fully
to be consumed by your children,
remaining always in our tabernacles,
offering Yourself day after day in Holy Mass.
How patient You are.
No gift so precious is so little appreciated.
You wait for us to come to You,
but we stay away.
You invite us to eat divine food,
but we prefer to starve.
You deserve our adoration
but we offer You indifference.
You teach me humility, Lord.
You who are Infinite Being
hide Yourself behind the appearance of the commonest food.
You who are adored by countless angels
remain alone, unhonoured, unrecognised.
How perfect, too, is your obedience.
Whenever I say the words of consecration
You obey and become really present.
If I place You on the tongue of one in grave sin
You do not withdraw your presence.
Here Lord, You are more approachable
than any of the officials around us.
We can come to You at any time, day or night.
You are always there.
We speak to You.
You speak silently into our hearts and minds.
You teach me poverty and detachment.
Here You are, more precious than any earthly treasure,
but You are prepared to live in the poorest chapel.
You teach me silence, Lord.
No matter how you are neglected, spurned or insulted
You never complain.
Lord, send your power from the sacred Host
to inspire me to live all these virtues
and every other virtue too.

123 MY MASS

Lord, only one thing will matter when I meet You
at the moment when You summon me for judgement.
That one thing will be the fervour of my love for You.
Love is your gift.
I am able to receive it only because You sacrificed Yourself for me.
Your Sacrifice continues in Holy Mass.
Your last supper, your death and the Mass
are all the one sacrifice.
It is infinite, inexhaustable.
Lord, deepen my faith.
Give me real, living conviction
that the Mass places really and actually present in our midst
that supreme action which You, Lord, consummated on Calvary.
It redeemed the world.
Your action on Calvary was not worth more than the Mass.
The two are but one and the selfsame sacrifice.
Your omnipotent hand pushes aside time and space,
I believe, Lord, that on Calvary and the Mass
You are the one infinite Priest and Victim.
Mass contains everything You, Lord, offered
and all that You acquired for men. I unite in all my Masses
everything I can offer,
my whole self, my thoughts, my words, my deeds.
I believe that I cannot offer Mass better
than in union with the Blessed Virgin
from whom You took the Body which You offered
and the Precious Blood You shed.
The sacrifice You offered on Calvary, my dear Jesus,
was only possible because your Mother had given her free consent.
Your will and the will of your blessed Mother
were totally united
I wish to unite myself with You, my dear Jesus.
Sharing in your priesthood I offer with You.
I wish also to be offered as a Victim of Love with You.
Lord, make my Masses ever more real.
Enliven my faith.
I believe that holy Mass should be my greatest act every day.
Fire my supernatural conviction.
Inspire it, invigorate it, stimulate it, vitalise it.

My Jesus, You gazed upon the world
as century followed century.
You saw your Church bring love of You to Europe.
You were honoured and loved in the age of great Saints.
Glorious cathedrals and beautiful churches have survived,
witnesses of how dedicated the people were.
Then came the tide of rebellion.
You know it all dear Lord.
I ponder it but I do not wish to detail it all.
That revolution against your eucharistic Sacrifice and Real Presence,
against the authority of your earthly Vicar,
against devotion to your blessed Mother
left Europe without the warmth of your love.
Ahead you saw another and even worse revolution—
Marxism, atheism, materialism, irreligion, immorality.
You made one last appeal.
You offered us a sign which could hardly be ignored.
You showed us your Heart, the symbol of your love,
a Heart surmounted by your cross,
pierced and bleeding, crowned with thorns,
a sign of suffering and rejected love.
Lord, You once said that no greater love was possible
than that which gave life for a friend.
I believe, Lord, You gave your life,
I believe that on the cross, You, a divine Person,
died because You loved us.
You plead for us to love You in return.
Jesus, I desire with all my being,
with all the yearning I am capable of,
to do just that.
But I want to do more.
I want to love You for all who do not love You.
I want to make reparation for sin.
I want to suffer for all the sinful pleasures in the world,
to pray for those who do not pray
to be good for those who are evil,
to believe and trust for all who do neither.
Lord, inspire me, guide me, lead me, stimulate me.

125   BEATING WITH LOVE

Within your breast, my Jesus,
the heart of the world beats with the very love of God.
Only to the little ones, the simple ones
are the sublime mysteries revealed
In your love You turn to those whose hearts are emptiest of self.
The wise and the learned may be too full to have room for you,
full of scientific and worldly knowledge .
Lord, let me never bring such an attitude to the reading of your word.
Too often it is discussed and dismissed like a curiosity.
Let me grasp it, embrace it, apply it to myself,
really live it.
Let me not waste time and effort discussing all possible meanings.
You mean your word to be accepted with simplicity.
You thanked your Father for hiding these things
from the learned and the clever
and revealing them to mere children (Matt. 11,25).
I long to be one of these little ones of yours
with whom You share your divine secrets.
You know my weakness; you understand it
with understanding founded on your own gentleness
and your lowliness before your Father. "Learn for me" you said,
"for I am gentle and humble in heart" (Matt. 11,29).
Yes, Lord, but I cannot learn from You
without your grace and your help.
Of myself I can do nothing.
So enlighten my whole being.
Endow me with the power to grasp at the heart,
the essential core of your message.
That heart is your Sacred Heart;
the sign of your limitless love.
I long to answer your call.
"Come to me" You say.
My search for God ends in You,
in the contemplation of your love.
Give me, Holy Spirit, your gift of understanding
to enable me to see with simplicity
the profoundity of your message of love.

Lord Jesus, I stand in spirit beneath your Cross
Your Heart no longer rises and falls.
The blood has ceased to flow from your wounds.
I see the spear open your side
and blood and water pour out.
Here is our unique source of life.
Your precious Blood has promised salvation for our race.
The water symbolizes your gift of baptism
by which your followers will be born again,
born to the new life
which is a sharing in your divine nature.
How great is the love, O Jesus, signified by your Heart.
That love made You embrace sorrow and suffering.
Your sufferings prove your love.
As that blood and water gush forth
a birth is taking place,
the birth of your other self,
your mystical Body,
your Church.
Another birth is happening too.
Your Mother is here, standing with me.
I heard You give her to John
and John to her.
Children of grace are born to the Mother of Sorrows.
Here is the mystery hidden in God
through all the ages.
What a mystery it is!
Help me, Lord, to understand it even as I say
that every Christian is born from the suffering of a God,
who loved us so much that He died for us.
Help me to lean over this unique spring of life
to draw from it with joy my salvation,
to love God, to love my fellows, to love all creation
with love springing from your opened Heart.
You continue to live out your personal drama, O Jesus,
in your Church, in our Mass
until the end of time.
O Lord, enable me to enter deliberately
into this personal drama of yours
to make it my own.

127 CONFIDENCE

My Jesus, You are all love.
You revealed your Sacred Heart to prove that love.
You are always the Good Shepherd watching over your flock.
I know, I believe with all my heart that I can do nothing
towards my sanctity or my salvation without You.
Gazing on your Heart, sign of love,
I resolve to live without anxiety.
I can place all my cares in You.
I look back on the trials of my life.
You have always been with me.
When I have faced frustrations and disappointments,
when I have been misrepresented and misunderstood,
when I have been let down by those I tried to help,
when I have been gravely ill
You have always been with me.
Teach me now never to look for happiness in creatures.
Many things please me, Lord, I know.
It would be dishonest to deny it.
You have made your creatures reflect your beauty.
But all are so limited.
I love the beauty of music and the charm of good art;
I marvel at the prodigies of science;
I appreciate the wonder of nature;
I thank you for the loveliness of the flowers.
But all these are soon exhausted.
I give myself wholly, in absolute trust to You.
I believe I cannot hope in You too much.
I cannot obtain less that I hope for from You.
You will uphold me against anything that threatens me.
You will always be with me to strengthen my weakness.
Let me always remember to contemplate your love.
I want to carry my hope as far as it can go.
Save me from both despair and presumption.
Hope is your gift, O loving Heart.
Give it to me in full measure.
Hide me in your depths.
Let nothing take away or weaken my trust.
I know that when I surrender myself to You
I am always on the safe road to Heaven.

What a fitting symbol of your love
is your Heart, O Jesus.
It is wounded by the proud, cruel multitude of our sins.
Others may have deserved such treatment,
but never You, O sinless Saviour.
I see the soldier piercing your Heart.
It was the sins of the world that put direction
and vigour into the hesitation of Longinus.
Man's sin sharpened the point of his spear.
But how the design of Providence is demonstrated here.
From your opened pierced Heart
the Church, your bride, is born.
That bleeding wound is the gate in the ark's side
put there for man's salvation.
From your Heart pour out seven streams,
torrents of never failing grace.
Now we can wash our soiled robes,
wash them in your Blood, O Lamb of God.
I sorrow, dear Lord, when I see those around me
returning to the sins which wounded your Heart.
You see this world, too, O divine Saviour.
Not one of your ten commandments is widely observed.
I weep for the sins of my world.
I try to see everything around me as You see it.
I see the media—the press, the radio, television, films, plays.
You see them too, dear Lord.
How terrible it is to realise that so many of those You love
for whom You suffered and died,
delight in being entertained by the vision of sin.
You plead for our love.
Instead we find pleasure in words and pictures
which try to portray as graphically as can be
the sin for which You died.
Lord, help me to convince people that the better course for them
is to reproduce in the burning love of their hearts
the flames that are the signs of the love of your Heart.
Yes, Lord, this is the grace I ask from You now.
May my devotion to your Sacred Heart be so fervent
that it will melt the hardest hearts
and kindle in all I meet the flame of your love.

129   CREATOR AND REDEEMER

How marvellous it is, Lord!
You, the Creator of all outside Yourself
show us your Heart to plead for our love.
O Sacred Heart of the divine Maker of all!
By You all things were made.
Without You nothing was made.
You are Light from your Father's light.
True God from true God.
You were compelled by love
to take a human body to be the second Adam.
Your love made You sacrifice Yourself
to restore what the first Adam had lost.
That love of yours,
which was the bountiful Creator of earth, sea and skies
took pity on our first parent's fall
and broke the chains that bound us.
That stream of glorious love
always flows from your Sacred Heart.
Never will it cease to flow.
How many millions of your human creatures
need the grace of pardon!
May all come to this well of your love,
your Sacred Heart, to draw it.
Lord, I look around our world now;
I think of it throughout the centuries.
I see the torrent of sin.
To make reparation for it all
your Heart was pierced by the lance.
To wash us from our sins
blood and water poured from it.
Yes, Lord, You, infinite Love
willed your Heart to be wounded
with a blow that disclosed its secrets
that we might revere the wounds
that are pledges of the love we cannot see.
Beneath this symbol of love You, infinite Victim
suffered in your Passion
and beneath it You offered your humble sacrifice.
Oh, how I long to love You in return!

Holy Spirit, you inspired St. Paul to write,
"The attitude you should have
is the one that Christ Jesus had:
He always had the nature of God
but He did not think that by force
He should try to become equal with God;
instead of this, of his own free will
He gave up all he had
and took the nature of a servant.
He became like man
and appeared in human likeness
He was humble and walked the path of obedience
all the way to death—
his death on the cross" (Phil. 2, 5-8).
The Apostle then tells us the result of this
"For this reason God raised Him
to the highest place above
and gave Him the name that is
greater than any other name.
And so, in honour of the name of Jesus
all beings in heaven, on earth and in the world below
will fall on their knees
and will openly proclaim that
Jesus Christ is Lord,
to the glory of God the Father" (Phil. 2, 9-11).
Holy Spirit, inflame me, penetrate me
with understanding of the inner meaning of obedience.
You inspired the author of the letter to the Hebrews to write:
"Even though He was God's Son, He learned
through his sufferings to be obedient" (Heb. 5,8).
In Gethsemane Jesus prayed,
"My Father, if it is possible
take this cup of suffering from Me!
Yet not what I want,
but what You want.
Your will be done" (Matt. 26, 39-42).
Holy Spirit, pour into my innermost being
a deep conviction that obedience lies at the heart of Christ's way.
Help me to radiate this conviction to those around me.

THE WAY OF OBEDIENCE

I ponder in your presence Lord, the words of St. Paul,
saying that if we surrender ourselves
to be slaves of obedience
the result will be to be right with God (Rom. 6, 16).
Disobedience, Lord, seems to reign to-day.
They call it freedom, or even democracy.
I see social life being ruined around me.
Without obedience to authority there is no order.
Lord, help those who are so confused
wandering like sheep without shepherds.
Lord, I beg You have mercy on those who rebel
and, worse still, invite or convince others to rebel.
Enlighten your children to understand that
your Church is a teacher, a divinely guided teacher,
and that obedience to its teaching
is the way of true wisdom,
You did not will your revealed truth
to be discovered by a majority vote.
True obedience comes from the heart.
Lord, help me to understand even more.
I recall the grief of St. Paul
when he discovered that the Galatians were disobedient;
"You were doing so well!
Who made you stop obeying the truth?
How did he persuade you?
It was not done by God.
Our life in union with the Lord
makes me confident that your elders
will not take a different view" (Gal. 5,10).
I thrill to read Peter's words to the High Priest,
"We must obey God, not men" (Acts 5,29).
Lord, lead your children now
along the ever safe path
of obedience to the authority
You have commissioned to teach in your name.
Curb the activity of those who are disloyal.
"The effects of loyalty will remain forever"
says your inspired word (Sir. 40,12).

Lord, I believe that prayer is the greatest
need of the Church, the world amd my own self.
I know the subtle attraction of the world around me.
It is dominated by the materialism, the secularism of the media.
Unless I force myself I cannot find time to pray.
Help me, Lord; give me strength of will
to make time, to leave the world,
to make a silent cloister of my mind
to contemplate You.
The modern world tries to make me cut You out.
It tries to fill the whole capacity of my mind
with itself, or myself.
I know I must make space for You;
You are the greater reality.
I can contemplate nothing more wonderful than You.
All around me seems to ignore You.
Yet You are everywhere.
The hurly-burly of life all happens in You.
Men sin in You.
They ignore You while existing in You.
How can I detach myself more from the world?
In the midst of all the noise
I seek the silence of contemplation.
In the midst of turmoil
I seek peace of mind.
The magnetism of materialism
opposes my efforts, to elevate my thoughts.
The visible tries to become
more real than the invisible.
Lord, in my heart of hearts I long
to be captivated by heavenly delights,
to thirst always and sigh gently
for a sense of your presence, infinite God.
Lord, I long to contemplate in silence
your majesty, your judgements,
your benefits, your promises.
Infinite Love, wonder of wonders,
stimulate me often to contemplate You,
consciously to live and think and love in You.

133 CHARITY

Lord, strengthen my conviction about the centrality of love.
You said that to love is your very own commandment.
I know I must love all my fellow human beings with
the same love with which I love You
The second Commandment is the same as the first.
Pour into my soul all the graces I need
to strengthen my love,
to make my love grow.
Deepen my faith to intensify my charity.
I believe I must see, love and serve You
in all those among whom I live.
Lord, help me to look on them all
as I would look on You,
that is an inferior regarding a superior.
Help me to discover You in everybody
even in those who are must unworthy.
I wish to make love, fervent love,
a real major, powerful sanctifying force in my life.
I believe that true love leads to peace.
Lord, help me, be with me always
so that I will live up to this conviction.
Help me, sweet Lord, to understand
how easily I can hurt others.
Help me to avoid the word or deed
that causes hurt or suffering.
Guide me to use words and do only those things
which promote love, peace and understanding.
Lord, make me a more caring person.
I shall try to forget myself
in my efforts to care for others.
Give me insight enough
to understand hidden anxieties and secret worries.
Breathe your word into my mind
to sacrifice my time and my comfort for others.
What an ideal You, O Lord, hold out to me!
"Love one another as I have loved You" (John 13,34).
Yes Lord, indeed, You gave your all, your life.
With your help I shall do the same.

O most Sacred Heart of Jesus
You long to shower your favours on all of us.
You invite me to become more like You
Help me to drive away from me always
feelings, desires and attractions which are opposed to You.
I want to reform my whole life
in so far as is necessary to be really like You.
But You, Lord, told me to learn of You
because You are meek and humble.
How wise You are, Lord.
You know that if only I can rid myself of pride
the way will be open for me to grow in every virtue.
Lord, help me at all times to restrain my anger.
Help me never to show annoyance or irritation.
May I always be fully master of myself.
Help me to keep calm in spite of frustrations
and especially when I am the victim
of the sins or shortcomings of others.
Help me to bear in silence and serenity
all the little humiliations which come to me,
without complaining or making excuses.
I never forget, Lord, that I deserve far more than I receive.
You know me through and through.
I have no secrets from You.
All my past sins are open to You.
Dear Lord, I thank you for having forgiven them.
But, let the memory of them keep me humble.
Jesus, my Lover, give me the grace to understand
that I am not always right.
Help me to see the real good in those who oppose me.
I know that when I have in the past lost control of myself
it has been because I have been too proud,
too ready to blame others and too easily to lose sympathy.
Yes, for the love of your Sacred Heart
I sincerely want to sacrifice all my self-love.
I want to nail it to the Cross with You.
I want to creep into your divine Heart
like a child coming to school again
to learn how to be really meek and humble.

135   TO JOHN THE BAPTIST

O John in heaven, who were privileged
to baptise God made Man,
your soul in your eternal home
sees Mary and thanks her,
for you know that it was she who brought Jesus to you.
Gabriel had told your father that from your very birth
you would be filled with the Holy Spirit.
When the Mother of Jesus visited your mother she said,
"Why should this great thing happen to me,
that my Lord's mother should come to visit me?
For as soon as I heard your greeting,
the baby within me jumped with gladness" (Luke, 43-44).
For eternity you must be thanking Mary for this favour.
The Holy Spirit was always with you.
You were standing by the River Jordan
with two of your disciples.
As you saw Jesus passing by, you said,
"There is the Lamb of God" (John 1,36).
They followed Jesus.
He turned and asked them
"What are you looking for?"
They answered, "Where do you live, Rabbi?"
"Come and see", He answered.
It was about four o'clock in the afternoon.
They spent the rest of the day with Him.
One of them was Andrew, Simon Peter's brother.
At once he found his brother Simon and told him,
"We have found the Messiah".
Then he took Simon to Christ
who looked at him and said.
"Your name is Simon, son of John,
but you will be called Cephas" (John 1, 41-42).
Yes, John, you were responsible
for introducing to God the Son his first earthly Vicar.
Mary brought her Jesus to you.
You brought Peter to Him.
One year later you gave your life for Christ.
Pray for me now, O blessed Precursor
that Mary will bring me ever closer to Him.

Jesus, by expressing my faith
in your real, true and substantial presence
in the Holy Eucharist
I strengthen it.
Your Heart reveals to me the mystery of your love.
You prove your love by giving Yourself to us
to feed the lives of our souls
and to remain with us always
in the Blessed Eucharist.
It is wonderful to be able to contemplate
your Sacred Heart as the sign of your love.
It is even more wonderful to be convinced
that that same Heart is always present in the Holy Eucharist.
Your Sacred Heart beats in me, touches me
when You feed me with your own Body and Blood.
You live with me, abide with me, govern me
in the Sacrament of your love.
You said, dearest Lord, that
when I eat your flesh and drink your blood
I abide in You
and You abide in me (John 6,57).
Help me to understand how You abide,
not by a mere passing visit but by a stable, permanent state.
When your physical presence within me
ceases after Holy Communion my blessed union with You continues.
You abide with me spiritually
by the irradiation of your Love.
Lord, I believe that your daily coming to me
nourishes, strengthens and consolidates
my union with You,
making it ever more profound
so that You can exert an ever greater influence over me.
That is the great favour I ask of your love.
I want to live at every moment
under the influence of your limitless love.
Never let me be separated from You, loving Lord,
but help me to intensify my loving union.

137 LOVE FOR LOVE

My Jesus you offer the image of your Sacred Heart to us
as a reminder to love You
in return for your love of us.
I know well all the proofs You have given
of your infinite love.
I look around me, Lord,
and I see how your infinite love is forgotten.
People live without thinking of You.
O what a terrible mystery it is!
Even those who are considered to be devout
give so very little of their time to You.
Even before the epidemic of vandalism
caused us to keep them closed
our churches were often empty.
So little prayer!
So little sacrifice!
So little thought of your Love!
"God is Love",
said your beloved Apostle (1 John 4,8).
Your love surpasses all knowledge (Eph. 3,19).
Yet so very few people seem to think of it.
During your life on earth
they laughed You to scorn.
Now, it seems, anything and everything
is more important then You, the tremendous Lover.
You know, dearest Jesus, how much I want to love You.
Teach me the most precious of sciences,
the science of your love.
The contemplation of the many proofs of your love
challenges me, stimulates me
to love You in return.
But what can I do?
I offer every moment of every day,
every task, every detail of my work to You.
I want each to be saturated in your love.
Enclose me, dear Lord, in the sanctuary of your Heart
which was opened by the lance.
Never let me forget your limitless love.
I want to give You my life in return for it.

Lord, your beloved Apostle was so inspired
to record that when You had died,
given your all, for love of us,
a soldier was permitted to open your side.
Blood and water poured out,
the price of our salvation,
springing from your Heart,
the sign of your love,
as from a mysterious fountain
giving power to the Sacraments of the Church
to bestow on us the life of grace,
which is a sharing in your divine nature.
What a stupendous mystery!
I thank You, Lord, for permitting me
to contemplate it
when the immense majority of the people
Your love has created
never even think of it.
The crowds in our streets,
on our summer beaches,
thronging our super-markets and stores—
O Lord, what are they missing?
Is this really the design of your Providence
that so few should be aware
of the mystery of your love?
I value it, dear Jesus,
more than the pearl of great price.
Is it your will that so very many
go through life ignorant of it?
Do you really intend all the little children
I see playing around me
to grow up immersed in the world of television
or of purely human concerns
but knowing nothing of these supreme mysteries?
How privileged I am, dear Lord.
I want to make your Heart my heart.
I am a member of your Body;
Lord, let me live with your life
always trying to return love for your infinite love.

139   WITH IRENAEUS

O Lord, in your love, wisdom and goodness
you use every means to help your Church.
I talk to you to-day about Saint Irenaeus.
Did he come from Smyrna?
Did he know St. Polycarp
a disciple of the beloved disciple?
In your providence he studied in Rome,
then became a priest at Lyons.
His name means "peace", the way to unity.
So when he brought a letter from Lyons to Rome
it urged leniency towards the Montanist heretics.
Irenaeus, Lord, became bishop of Lyons
his predecessor having been martyred.
Lord, your Church was still taking its first smallish steps.
You raised up Irenaeus to teach that you are one,
the same in the New Testament as in the Old.
He insisted that You, Father,
are one with your divine Son
in your work of Revelation and Redemption.
You willed, O Lord, that Irenaeus
should stress the importance of tradition.
Guide the people of to-day, Lord,
to accept the apostolic succession of the Church's hierarchy.
Teach them the truth about the Bible,
the collection of books inspired by You.
Dispel, O good Lord, ignorance
about how the Canon of your revealed word in holy Writ came to be.
I thank you, Lord, for giving Irenaeus to your Church
to teach the truth about the authority
of the Four Gospels.
To-day Lord, we are able to learn
that the Church of Irenaeus believed
that to discover the truth they had
to discover the teaching of the Church
founded in Rome by Peter and Paul.
Lord, I thank You for allowing me
to discover the importance of Irenaeus,
your Bishop of Peace and Reconciliation.

I think to-day, dear Lord,
of those who established your Church
not only by their apostolic labours
but by their blood.
I pray now for greater love of your Church.
It is indeed a mystery of faith.
I see it in our world now—
far outnumbering all the members of the sects put together.
Its marks are miraculous.
Lord, how people differ,
in colour and in tongue,
in the heritage of their nations
in the distinctions of their classes,
in the multitude of their ways of life.
Yet they all worship in the Catholic way,
all believe Catholic truth,
all obey the one Catholic authority
under the successor of blessed Peter.
How wonderful it is to be a child of the Church.
But, why O God, is it that members of your Church
are still so few
when compared with all the people of the world?
The answer lies hidden in your infinite Wisdom.
Make me, Lord, like Peter,
a firm solid rock of immovable faith.
Lord, strengthen our Pope to-day.
Pour your grace into the minds and hearts of more people
to proclaim their complete loyalty to him.
Too many are like sheep without a shepherd.
Rome is always there.
History reveals it like a beacon of light.
Why do You permit so few to recognise it?
Your world needs the Church, O Lord.
Enlighten your Vicar that more will turn to him.
Enlighten the enemies of the Church, move those who are indifferent
that they may be converted to You.
Bring back those who have strayed.
Give me strength to work even more
for the glory of your one, true Church.

141 ST. PAUL

I thank You, God, for giving the world St. Paul.
He was one of your greatest miracles.
Yet, how people forget now
his marvellous conversion on the road to Damascus.
What a mighty heart You gave him!
I think of him now, Lord,
always suffering, always opposed, always harassed
yet travelling on and on
carrying your good tidings with him,
always reasonable, always methodical,
determined to plant the Gospel seed
in city after city, opening up a royal road,
a triumphant highway
to the very limits of the western world.
Lord, give me something, just a little, of St. Paul's spirit.
May I. like him, find my repose and my peace
in the love of Christ.
May I seek above all the approbation of God.
Fill me, Lord, with your graces,
of generosity, of devotedness, of self-forgetfulness,
that I may always be able to raise myself
far above the preoccupations of self-interest and vanity.
Lord, I want to be able to win affection
by showing affection.
I want to win affection
not to be loved for my own comfort
but because I know
that if folk like me, I shall be able to help them.
Yes, Lord, I want to be a magnet for souls.
Keep me always gentle, genuine and sympathetic,
never austere and aloof.
Give me, like St. Paul, a heart that is on fire.
Make me uncompromising with error
but at the same time considerate and understanding.
Make me like a mother
who warms her children with her caresses.
Convince me, at the same time,
to run to meet the Cross
and embrace it with love.
Blessed Paul, obtain for me a heart and spirit like yours.

142   PRECIOUS BLOOD

O my beloved Redeemer,
to-day I talk with you about the Blood You shed.
You had to embrace our human nature to have it.
Then, shedding it, You gave it back to us.
It was the price of our redemption.
St. Peter called the blood You shed, precious (1 Peter 1,19).
Indeed it is, dear Lord, but how generously You gave it.
I think of that first shedding when You were circumcised.
How terrible must have been your sweat of blood,
when the price of our redemption
mixed with the soil of Gethsemane.
The soldiers scourges must have been soaked with it.
It must have covered the pillar,
flowed to the ground and spotted the walls.
I think of it shed as You were so cruelly crowned with thorns,
as You fell and were beaten on the way to Calvary,
and as they nailed You to the Cross.
O Jesus, You accepted all this agony.
You embraced it with love
to make satisfaction for all human sin.
Now, Lord, I want to unite with your sufferings
the tiny mite of my own,
the pains of illness and daily work,
the frustrations, disappointments, failures and anxieties.
You took your Precious Blood from the heart of your Mother.
In your body it became precious beyond description,
every drop of it infinitely adorable.
Lord, do cause your Precious divine Blood
to pour drop by drop
into the hearts of those who have wandered from You.
May it soften their hardness;
may it warm them into loving You again.
Lord, irrigate the field and garden of your Church
with your Precious Blood.
May great Saints and apostles rise again
to bring knowledge and love of You to our world.
Sweet Jesus, the entire stream of your divine Blood
is on the altar at every Mass.
It is in every consecrated Host, Lord, everywhere in the world.
O Lord, awaken people everywhere to love this sublime truth.

143 TO ABIDE IN CHRIST

Jesus, I read to-day how You said to your Apostles,
"Abide in Me and I in You" (John 15,4)
I know that without your constant help I cannot do this.
But this is my wish.
"He who eats Me, You said
"abides in Me and I in him" (John 6,57).
When You come to me in Holy Communion
You do not leave
without having impressed on my soul
the warmth of your love.
You said, Lord, that you are come
"to cast fire on the earth and
what will I but that it be kindled?" (Luke 12,49).
Light the fire of your love dearest Jesus,
in my soul where You find hospitality.
I know this happens, my Lord,
but I should be more vividly aware of it.
I want to live my union with You
in its complete fullness.
Pour your grace into my inner being, Lord,
to deepen and cement my union with You.
How the world crowds in on me!
It seems to have a bewitching magnetism of its own.
Those who want to enrich themselves
make their goods so attractive
that they are hard to resist.
Lord, You know that this fact
lies at the heart of commerce.
Help me, my most powerful and loving Friend,
to resist the temptation to spend my time
in pleasure, enjoyment and relaxation.
I want You to be my world,
not television or the press or secular books.
So, dear Jesus, consume by your love
everything in my desires which keeps me away from You.
I so long to flee away
from whatever makes me love You less
or diminishes my power to abide in You.

O Jesus, You told us that your own special commandment
is that we love one another.
You said that people would know whether we are your disciples
from the degree of our love for one another.
You have revealed that it is by treating our fellows
as we would treat You that we shall be judged.
Love, O Lord, is your gift.
As a child at school I learned that I cannot take a step
towards my salvation without your grace.
Give me your very special grace to love all my fellow men
in the way and to the extent You will.
If I truly love them I will try to share my treasures with them.
Holy Spirit, give me spiritual insight and understanding
to know what real charity is.
Give me the courage and zeal to practise it.
All around me I see thousands, millions,
who are sick and poor.
Some there are who are physically sick or materially poor.
Yes Lord, it is fairly easy to help them.
But spiritual sickness and religious poverty abound.
Lord Jesus, why is it that so few of those who love You
are so slow, even reluctant, to share their faith?
You must know, dear Lord, I do not.
Can You not stir up in your Church, everywhere,
among bishops and priests and the laity
a lively sense of responsibility for those without faith?
Pour into every heart, dear Lord, the spirit of love,
of love which moves those who enjoy the treasures of your Church
to try to share them with those who are without them.
Lord, take away the blindness which seems to prevent so many
from seeing the spiritual starvation which surrounds them.
Lord,give members of your Church such a deep vivid conviction
that this is the one and only true Church
that they will move mountains to lead others to it.
Take away the ignorance which proclaims
that one religion is as good as another.
Remove the false irenicism which kills the sense of mission.
In your grace drive all who love You to obey your call,
"Go out into the whole world
and preach the Gospel to every creature" (Mark 16,15).

145   LONGING FOR LOVE

O Heart of Jesus, I love You.
You are the symbol God Incarnate chose
of his limitless love for me.
That love, O Lord, is beyong my understanding.
In your infinite wisdom and love You chose to create me.
You knew how very unworthy and sinful I would be.
My whole life is present to your eternal gaze.
Yet, knowing this, You brought me out of nothing
instead of the great Saint You might have created.
How strange that after that and after countless other benefits
You had to tell me to love You.
O Jesus, strengthen my faith, my conviction,
my supernatural realisation of all You have done for me.
Had You not commanded it
I hope I would still have longed to love You
with all my heart,
with all my soul,
with all my mind,
with all my strength.
Loving Jesus, I long to love You,
above all honours and possessions,
above all enjoyments and pleasures,
more than all my relatives and friends,
more than anything that belongs to me,
more than myself.
Jesus, I long to love You just for Yourself
because You are goodness without limit,
infinitely worthy of being loved.
Lord Jesus, light up within me a living conviction
of the immensity of your love for me.
Not only did You create me,
You became man for me; You gave me your teaching;
You showed me how the infinite God would live a human life,
You suffered and died for me and rose from death.
You gave me your Church to teach me.
You continue to give me yourself through your Church.
You preserved for me the supreme moment of your earthly life.
You come to me daily in Holy Communion.
You forgive me over and over again.
You have made your Mother, my Mother.
O Jesus, I long to love You in return for your loving me.

146   BECOMING A VICTIM

Lord, your Holy Spirit tells me
that You humbled Yourself and became obedient unto death,
even to death on the Cross.
For which cause God exalted You
and gave You a name which is above every other name.
I know, dear Jesus, that I am proud.
I am very conscious of my lack of humility.
I beg You to help me by your constant grace
to live as I believe.
You know how firmly I believe that
obedience to lawful authority
is obedience to your will.
I believe that You will to make known your will to me
through the directives of those in authority over me.
You know how sincerely I wish to be obedient.
Help me to acquire the necessary humility.
You, infinite God, became a child.
You obeyed your Foster-Father and your Mother.
You obeyed the laws of your time.
You went down to Nazareth
and were subject to your earthly parents,
even though You knew You had created them.
On this very point St. Paul tells me,
"Let that mind be in you which is in Christ Jesus" (Phil. 2,5).
Yes, Lord, I long for the security of dwelling in your will.
To attain this I pray for your help to abandon my own will
to embrace the divine will.
Deepen my conviction that supernatural obedience
places me in direct contact with that divine will, your will, Lord,
and that if I leave the path of obedience
I leave the secure road of your will
for the dangerous way of my own will.
I trust in your government
through the commandments of those in authority.
You, dear Lord, prefer obedience to penance or anything else.
I believe it is the shortest path to union with the eternal Father.
You redeemed the world by becoming a Victim of love.
I become a victim by loving obedience,
the complete immolation of myself in your honour.
Enable me to see your will—the sacrament of every moment.

I think, Lord, about the influence of St Benedict.
How did the followers of that one man
become so numerous, so influential?
Under your mysterious Providence
they seem to have been one of the greatest forces
in bringing your truth to Europe.
"To work is to pray", St. Benedict proclaimed.
Lord, convince me even more of this truth.
I want to offer all my work to You.
I long to make a perfect gift.
But it is hard to oppose the attitude around me
that work is something to be avoided,
to be done as little as possible.
Yes, Master, I think of You and your Foster-Father.
Your example inspired St. Benedict.
But my world thinks otherwise—completely.
When I work hard I am mocked, even threatened.
Still, Lord, in spite of everything I must try.
I want my every job, every working hour
to be a gift for You,
and a gift that is worthy.
I am thinking of the sons of Benedict
building monasteries and churches and cathedrals,
cultivating the land, educating in art and culture,
setting such an example of liturgical prayer.
Lord, make me live up to my deep conviction
that praising You is essential if I am to be holy.
You inspired David and others to compose the psalms.
In your Providence You willed that they should come down to us.
When I use them in my prayer
I hear them telling me about and exalting your perfections, O God.
They express my needs; they enlighten my mind.
Holy Spirit give me more of your precious gift of understanding
so that I shall be able to penetrate their inmost meaning.
Yes, Lord, Benedict's mission was one of peace.
Give me tranquillity of soul.
Teach me to rise above all that cause me anxiety.
May I remember that I am always in your love.

O Lord, I thank you to-day for giving us the Saints.
Together they are like a beautiful mosaic depicting every virtue.
St. Camillus saw You in all who are suffering.
Lord, help me to be like him.
So often I see the aged and the lonely.
But when I try to obtain help for them it is impossible.
Lord, enlighten the minds of those responsible for our social order.
Let them see where help is most needed.
I am distressed, Lord,
I could weep now in your presence
at the vision of so many beds being occupied,
so much money being spent,
and so much care devoted
to the murder of unborn children.
Lord, You are all powerful.
Take away the resistance of men's wills to what is right.
Have all your children see the folly
of spending millions of pounds on weapons of destruction.
Restore among people everywhere
a deep sense of respect for life,
a realisation that in serving those in need
they are serving You.
Dear Jesus, flash into the minds and hearts of all peoples
the message of love You gave to your Apostles
between your last supper and your agony.
Yes, Lord, fire my own zeal, too.
Spiritual sickness may be worse than bodily disease,
I live among those whose spiritual state does not exist.
It is absolutely negative.
You know, dear Jesus, that in these days
a majority of those for whom You died
rarely think of You or pray to You.
They do not know You in Yourself.
How can they see You in the people around them?
We need, Lord, an about turn.
Charity must supplant expediency.
Direct at least the minds of those who love You
so that, by setting an example to those around them
they may contribute to the reforms and rethinking
which our society so much needs.

149 ST. BONAVENTURE

Lord, I think of you now as I think St. Bonaventure did.
You are the way, he proclaimed.
You are the door.
By You, Lord we mount,
by You we are borne.
Yes I cannot too often gaze on You hanging on your Cross.
I look with faith,
believing that You are indeed my God,
giving your life for love of me.
I gaze on You with hope, love and wonder,
with joy and appreciation,
with praise and jubilation.
Promise me, Lord as You promised the thief from your Cross,
that I shall live with You in paradise.
I long to turn the very apex of my soul to You,
to be entirely transformed in You.
Penetrate me ever more and more
by the fire of the Holy Spirit,
the fire You sent on earth.
I ask this, Lord, of grace, not of learning;
I ask it of desire, not of understanding;
I ask it of earnest prayer, not of attentive reading.
I ask it of You, my Lord and my God.
Only You, and no man, can give it.
I ask it of darkness, not of radiance.
I ask it not of light
but of a fire that inflames me completely,
and with extreme sweetness and burning affection
transports me to You, my God.
I want to silence my cares, my limits, my dreams.
I want to be united with You, my Lord,
as I gaze upon You hanging on your Cross.
With You, O Jesus, I will pass out of this world to the Father.
Yes, I look around my world.
Everything that is good or true or beautiful
takes me to You.
My Jesus, I want to belong entirely to You.
I want You to magnetise me
so that I shall never leave the embrace of your love.

150 MARY OF CARMEL

What a wonder of the Church, Lord, is the Order of Carmel.
It is your Blessed Mother's own Order.
How St. Theresa loved her!
Like her, dear Lord, I want to live totally consecrated to your Mother.
My work must be her work,
my thoughts, her thoughts,
my prayers, her prayers,
my wishes, her wishes.
Sweet Mother Mary, I turn to You now.
I know I must be austere because I must live apart from the world.
I mean that my life must be heavenly rather than earthly.
Then teach me how to mix gentleness with austerity,
how to temper severity with warmth.
May my union with you make my crosses attractive.
Make me ever more conscious of your mother-love.
Like St. Theresa I want my devotion to you to be
rich and strong, simple and childlike, loving and reverential.
Teach me like the mother you are
how I should honour you,
how I should pray to you,
how I should live in union with you.
Mother, always be near to me.
Help me to feel that you are near.
I do not wish my devotion to you to be remote.
I want it to be close and intimate.
Inspire me to celebrate each of your feasts
in the way you wish them to be celebrated.
Take away from my devotion to you, Mother,
everything that savours of routine.
I know you love me as the most perfect of mothers.
Perhaps emotion and feeling are misleading,
but, Mother, how can I really love you
without feeling near to you?
Pray for me; obtain very special graces for me.
Come into my life.
Be with me always.
Teach me humility, faith and surrender to God's will.
Inspire me to love those around me as you love them.
Teach me the secret of how to win everybody over
to believe in God, your Jesus and the Church.

151   HEAVENLY FATHER

The more I meditate on your infinite attributes, O God,
the more I realise how wonderful it is
to be not only your creature but your child.
I thank You, Lord, for creating me
rather than the other human beings You could have created
instead of me and destined for eternal life with You.
If I were only your creature I could never thank You enough.
But I am infinitely more.
I am really your child,
a sharer in your divine nature,
able to know as You know
and to love as You love.
You do even more for me, more than I can describe.
You became man and lived to show me how to live.
You gave me your infinitely wise teaching.
You suffered and died for me.
You gave me your Church and all it means.
Your Church to teach me always;
your Church to give me the life of your grace;
your Church to continue your one infinite sacrifice;
your Church to give me Yourself to feed my soul's life
and to be always in the tabernacle.
Your Church to forgive me when I sin.
Your Church to enrich humanity with your Saints.
You gave me your own Mother to be my Mother.
Loving Father, what more could You do?
And how inadequate has been my response.
I know I am proud and self-centred;
but, Father, help me to grow in humility.
Help me to be really and truly in every detail of my life
a little child.
That was your command.
Jesus, Lord, you thanked your Father
for hiding "those things from the wise and learned
and revealing them to little ones" (Matt. 11,25).
Father, keep me always in the way
of spiritual childhood and self-surrender.
May I always ponder with love and gratitude
this profound mystery—that You, infinite God
are my Father and I really your child.

152 TO BE A CHILD

O Infinite Lord of Lords, You have willed to be my Father.
You can make me live as your child.
Please do so.
I long to be loving, devoted, obedient, humble,
ever marvelling at the manifestations of your love.
Create in me the heart of a child,
filled with the reverence and awe of a child
but also filled with simple love.
Give me a heart with just one desire,
to abandon myself entirely to You
and every manifestation of your will.
May your will be always my will,
my honour, my consuming passion.
Help me to seek your will,
to love it, embrace it and adore it.
From all eternity I have been in your mind.
You know me now;
You know every detail
of what will happen to me in the future.
This consoles and comforts me now.
I firmly believe that in You,
infinite Love, I live and move and exist.
Whatever may happen to me is the gift of your love.
Grant that I may always accept it as such.
If You send me illness and pain,
blindness, deafness or incapacity,
never allow me to forget that
whatever it is, it must be the gift of your love.
Yes, my dear Father, I want to seek You
and to find You in everything
that comes to me, apart from my own choice,
no matter how hard it may be,
Father, preserve this spirit of sincerity in me.
May I never complain about what befalls me.
May I always long, as I do now,
to embrace You and to be embraced by You.
Truly, believe me, dearest Father,
more than anything else
I want to be one of your closest, most intimate friends.
Never let me think otherwise.

153   GRATITUDE

Lord, I honestly wish to make my whole life
a song of thanksgiving to You.
I believe that You, who know everything,
know that deep down in my heart I am grateful
for all You have done for me,
more than I can ever tell You in my prayers.
As your beloved disciple said of your earthly doings,
all the books in the world cannot contain,
are not big enough to hold
adequate descriptions of all Your love has given me.
I trust that my gratitude
will attract new graces, new gifts from You,
that it will draw upon me
even more your infinite liberality.
Help me to make my gratitude always more sincere.
I know how really poor I am.
I can never forget my sins,
how prone to evil I still am.
So often I want to think of You, Lord,
and the things of heaven,
especially your blessed Mother.
But I find my thoughts drawn to far less worthy concerns,
some of them even dangerous and sinful.
I believe that a more fervent spirit of thankfulness
will help me to live in your presence.
Lord Almighty, I want my understanding
of your infinite attributes to grow.
I want to comprehend more and more
the infinity of your love, wisdom, goodness, eternity and immensity.
I ask You, Lord, to give me this comprehension
through my conscious gratitude to You.
All my good longings are your gift.
I can never thank You enough.
I repeat again the longing I have
to make my whole life a song of thanksgiving to You.
I can do this only if You constantly help me.
I beg You, loving Father, to do this.

154   JESUS, MY LIFE

Jesus, if You had not died for me
I would be unable to look forward to life with You.
You called Yourself "the Life".
That You are indeed.
Infinite God, as You are, You have given me your life.
When I was baptised I was born again.
I received Your life.
When You come to me in Holy Communion
I receive You who are Life.
Sin is death.
When You have forgiven my sins
You have replaced death by life.
Lord, I look around me.
You once told us not to judge others
or we would be judged ourselves.
Only You, Lord, know the guilt of your children.
But so many of those You have created
seem never to think of You.
You are the greatest figure in all human history
but they disregard You
You gave us your Church
which brought your Way, your civilization to the world
but the majority of people seem to disregard it.
Indeed, how many treat your Church,
your channel of life to men
as your contemporaries treated You.
They laughed You to scorn.
Lord, Way, Truth and Life,
I want to live your life
so intensely, so fervently, so unfailingly
to make reparation to You
for all who never think of You,
especially for all who scorn You.
Lord, You are all powerful.
Move our humanity towards the truth
that they will cease to regard as "thinkers"
those who reject You, the life of the world.
Restore true wisdom to our race.
Be merciful. Transform the reign of death
into a kingdom of true life.

155 GRACE TO PRAY

Lord Jesus, You know how I long to pray well.
I know that if I am to penetrate the world around me
I must be a living monstrance, carrying You.
I want to pray more and to pray well
because I know that without prayer I cannot love You.
I cannot possess You.
I cannot reveal You.
Yes, dearest Lord, when I pray
I want to exchange thoughts with You,
I want to open myself to You,
to tell You of all my ambitions, my desires, my ideals.
You know already what they are.
I know what I would like them to be.
But they are so defective, so flawed, so beyond reality.
You know, too, Lord, that You are always in my mind.
I try to live in your presence.
But I have such a long way to go.
Help me, dear Lord, just to be able to pray sincerely.
Here and now I consecrate myself again to You.
I surrender my will to your will.
I want to praise You as worthily, as fittingly as I should.
I can never praise You enough or as You deserve.
The very thought of your infinite attributes overwhelms me.
But it consoles me, too.
I know that I, a poor sinner,
can never worthily or adequately adore your infinite majesty.
I bow down in spirit before it.
I want to make reparation for all those who never think of You,
as well as all those who deliberately sin against You.
I thank You, dear Lord, for the infinity of your love and mercy,
for the countless good things I owe to You.
I beg You, Lord, to pour your helps and graces
into my poor, unworthy, disloyal sinful soul.
Yes, Lord, in my prayer now
I want to rehearse my occupation for eternity.
Help me to put aside all my cares and worries
to give myself wholly to You.
I long for this so very much
because this is what You deserve, infinite, tremendous Lover.

F

Mary Magdalen in heaven, I turn to you to-day.
I think of you as so many people do—
as the reformed, penitent prostitute.
How you were magnetised by your contact with Jesus!
Christians of every age and place have been encouraged by you.
I think of the inspired words,
"Though your sins are like scarlet,
they shall be white as snow;
though they are red like crimson,
they shall become like wool" (Isaiah, 1,18).
Pray to-day, as the world honours you, for all sinners.
Pray for all who do not know Jesus.
Pray for all for whom his Resurrection means nothing.
but above all, pray that your beloved Jesus
will offer the grace of firm faith to a multitude of souls.
He made you the first herald of Easter joy.
You would not leave his grave
even after his disciples had gone away.
You continued seeking Him whom you could not find.
In tears you kept searching.
Pray for me that I may never cease to search for Jesus.
Because you persevered in searching,
you alone saw Him,
you who had remained behind to seek Him.
Ask your Jesus to give me the graces of love and perseverance.
May I be like you, Mary,
growing in love of Jesus day by day
as I persevere in seeking Him.
First of all Jesus called you "Woman".
You did not recognise Him.
Then He called you "Mary",
Lord, may I always remember
that your love for me is personal, intimate, individual.
You said, "I know my sheep" (John 10,14).
You know me Lord exactly as I am, through and through.
You know my sins, forgive them I beg You.
You know my weaknesses; strengthen them I pray.
You know my longings, my desires; purify and enlighten them.
Lord, I want to be all yours,
to love You as Mary Magdalen did.

157   **WITH GOD**

I have come to You, loving Father,
to talk to You as your child.
That is what I know I am.
But I want to love You as your child,
to trust You as your child,
to obey You as your child.
Speak to me, Father, now.
I pause to listen . . . .
It seems to be so hypocritical
to tell You that I really want to be a saint.
Yet I do.
I who am so full of self, so very proud,
so resentful if anything seems to go against me,
so immersed in my own concerns.
Lord, love is your gift.
I depend on You for it.
Give it to me in good measure,
pressed down, overflowing.
Here and now, Lord, I give You to-day.
I give You all the days that may lie ahead for me.
They may not be many.
You know; I do not.
But Lord, grant that when You call me
I shall be ready, in your grace and your love.
I am full of ideals.
I fall so very far short.
You know me, loving Father, through and through.
You know every minute of my day.
You know how work presses.
I pray now; I am writing this prayer
because at least this is proof that I do try to find time for You.
Give me all the graces I need
to do well all I have to do.
Help me to keep my mind always turned in the right direction.
Keep me like a compass needle
pointing always to You my magnetic pole.
Help me to put everything in my life,
every tiniest detail in the right context,
that is in the thought of You being ever present
and of being always abandoned to your Will.

Dear Lord, may I always keep my gaze on You.
May I never cease to move spiritually towards You.
I know that a gaze on You,
contemplation of You,
can never be exhausted.
I can never comprehend your limitlessness,
your timelessness, your immensity, your attributes.
I long to see You with the minds of the angels,
to see You as the greatest of the Saints saw You.
You are indeed an endless, infinite panorama of beauty.
I contemplate You—my God, my All.
Then I contemplate myself—so weak, so imperfect.
You, Lord, know me, see me, through and through.
I want to contemplate You with complete simplicity.
I want to see everything, especially myself, in You.
I believe, dearest Lord, that to surrender to your love,
to live in your love, is the surest way to conquer myself.
I want to be absorbed by You, in You.
Give me your help in putting your interests first in my thoughts.
Your communication is with the simple (Prov. 3,32).
Fill my mind, Lord, fill all its capacity
undividedly with attention to You.
I know I must think about many things
but I must place them all in You.
You are the universal context.
I sincerely wish—do believe me, Lord—
for everything in my mind to be illuminated
by just one source of light,
the light of my undivided absorption in You.
Give me, Lord, uprightness, honesty, candour,
  fidelity, the simplicity of a child,
with no artifices, no dissimulation.
I want to think of You, Lord, in goodness
and to seek You in simplicity of heart.
My Jesus, You were absorbed in your Father's work.
Only with your grace Lord, can I be like You.
Endow me with the simplicity which permits limpid souls
to enter the heights of God.
My one desire is to cast my heart into You, my God

159 LOVE FOR ALL

Lord, you have told us that there is only one love.
We are to love our neighbour
with the love with which we love You
I beg You now to guide me to see You in everybody I meet.
This means that I must sincerely try
to see everybody as my superior, as You, infinite God.
Help me to penetrate the mystery.
Help me to love the person whom I tend to dislike most
as I would love You.
Help me to see You imprisoned in the greatest sinner
and to release You by my love.
Inspire me to understand others,
to be able to put myself in their place.
Remind me when others hurt me never to seek revenge,
never to retaliate in anger,
but to accept the hurt with humility,
as You did in your Passion.
My wish, O Jesus, is to keep your example before me.
You were laughed to scorn but You did not retaliate in anger.
The hurt I receive is surely less than the hurt my sins deserve,
O Jesus, You know that I sincerely wish to obey You
when You say to me, "Judge not, and you shall not be judged"
(Luke 6,37).
Remind me always, Lord, especially when I am tempted to judge
that I cannot know the graces others receive
or how they accept or reject them.
Help me to see myself as I am in your sight,
all my sins, all my shortcomings, all my imperfections,
all the graces I have rejected.
Then I shall know that I cannot worthily judge others.
Those I guide may have reponded to your graces far better than I.
Positively, Lord, move me, inspire me,
give me the courage to speak or act when true love demands it.
You know, dear Jesus, when a kindly, encouraging word
will be effective.
You know how so many people suffer from a sense of neglect
and need just a helping hand.
Move me by your special grace to do what is needed
to lead back to You those who have strayed,
to bring to your truth those who have never known it.
In a word, dear Jesus, may I live always in love.

160 ST. IGNATIUS

I read to-day, Lord, about Ignatius of Loyola.
His spiritual appetite was awakened
by his reading the lives of the Saints.
Lord, let me never be so proud as to despise your Saints.
Rather, may I always look to them, day by day,
for example, encouragement and inspiration.
I believe, O God, that without You I can do nothing.
So like St Ignatius I turn to You.
He went first of all to your blessed Mother at Montserrat.
I give myself to you now, sweet Mother,
so that you will give me to your Son.
By your prayer obtain for me the virtues of Ignatius,
prudence, charity, gentleness, zeal for souls and for the Church.
Mother Mary, every word of yours recorded in the Gospels
tells of your obedience to the will of God.
St. Ignatius built his spiritual edifice on this foundation.
Lord, Jesus, you said that your meat was
to do the will of Him who sent You (John 4,34).
In Gethsemane You prayed
"not my will but thine be done" (Luke 22,42).
Teach me, Lord Jesus, as you inspired Ignatius to learn
that if peace of mind is desired
one must try to be perfect in obedience.
May I be comforted and sustained
by my desire and my efforts to seek and obey
your will in everything and always.
I consecrate to You, O Lord, my understanding and my will,
your most excellent and precious gifts.
Yes, Lord, I desire to be a holocaust of love for You
by the perfection of my surrender to your will.
For your love I want to overcome myself completely.
May my obedience to your will, be prompt and ready.
Give me that true humility to which nothing is difficult.
Give me that true meekness unto which nothing is hard.
Ignatius, pray for me that I may reflect your spirit.
Pray for the Society you founded,
that its members will always and everywhere
inspire those who know them
with true loyalty in everything to holy Mother Church.

Lord, God, Father, may I never forget that eternity is near.
Time is passing. I am passing with it.
Each moment brings me nearer to your judgement.
Keep me detached from everything that is earthly and passing.
Never allow me to forget that the task of preparing my soul
is with my always.
When You call me, Lord, only one thing will matter,
the intensity of my love for You.
Love is your gift, dear heavenly Father.
Pour it into my inmost being.
Forgive all my past sins and infidelities.
Fill me with the treasure which will increase my capacity
to comprehend You, Lord, when I see You.
Take away from me whatever will be an embarrassment then.
Comfort and consolation of spirit help me now.
But if You send me desolation and suffering
I accept them as your loving Will.
Enrich my soul now, dear Father.
Increase my capacity to know and love You in heaven.
Help me to anticipate my life with You in beatitude.
I try to contemplate the countless choirs of angels.
I long to meet the great company of the Saints, your lovers,
those who lived for You and died for You.
I long above all, dear Master,
to meet our lovely Mother, yours and mine.
I thank You once again for giving her to me
and me to her.
Yes, Lord, I know all these truths in my heart.
Help me to realise them vividly.
Give me deep, living conviction about eternity.
Be with me as the moments and days and weeks pass by.
Honestly, Lord, I wish to waste none of the time
You have given me in which to prepare to meet You.
But I know only too well that without You I am helpless,
incapable of a single fervent prayer or good deed.
Be with me, Lord, as I continue on my pilgrim way.
I long to love You fervently.
Mary dearest Mother, take me
with all I am and all I have.
Present me to your dear Son.

Jesus, I thank You for to-day's feast.
You loved your Mother so much
that You wished her to be honoured
always and everywhere in your Church
and especially at its centre, Rome.
In your divine loving Providence
You permitted the legend of the miraculous fall of snow
to inspire devotion for centuries
and to be celebrated in the Liturgy.
The whole Church thanks You, Lord, to-day
for causing the beautiful basilica to be built
to recall to the minds of all who see it
or celebrate the anniversary of its dedication
the Council of Ephesus and the solemn definition
of your blessed Mother's divine Motherhood.
You willed also, dear Lord, for the beauty of this Church
to witness to the fact that throughout the centuries
your Church has been proud to honour your Mother,
and to express that honour in the beauty of art.
I thank You, dear Lord, for permitting me
to be present in this first church of your Mother
on Christmas night to witness the procession
of the remains of the crib in which you were placed at Bethlehem.
I thank You, too, for permitting me
to visit and venerate the ancient icon of your Mother,
"the health or well-being, of the Roman people".
Dear Lord Jesus, I beg You give me the grace
to grow in devotion to your Virgin Mother.
You know how I have dedicated myself
to You through her.
From You, through her, I believe, will come
all the help I need to live my consecration.
To your Mother I say in my heart at all times,
"I am all thine, my Queen, my Mother,
and all that I have is thine".
As I contemplate all that is signified in to-day's feast,
in the traditions You willed to be associated
with the first wonderful Church of your Mother,
I renew as fervently as I can
my consecration to You through her.

163   THE TRANSFIGURATION

To-day, Lord, I pray with You
about the divine confirmation on the hilltop of your Godhead.
Peter's faith was confirmed
as he saw your dazzling appearance,
as, for a moment, your divine nature
shone out through your mortal body.
Your eternal Father's voice out of the cloud,
the symbol of his presence during the forty years in the wilderness
must have remained in his memory for all his life.
You had with You, Lord, the same three Apostles
who were to witness You in agony in Gethsemane.
You willed now to strengthen their faith
to withstand your passion and death.
Strengthen my faith to-day, dear Lord,
that amid the materialism and irreligion which surround me
I may always believe without the slightest doubt.
Moses and Elias spoke about your death.
You were transfigured, Lord, to remove the scandal of the Cross.
Your eternal Father revealed his special presence on the mountain
by a supernatural light and whiteness as dazzling as light.
I beg You who made the sun and all light
to enlighten my mind with vivid faith.
Penetrate the dark and hidden places.
Help me to comprehend the deepest meaning
of all You have revealed.
Faith will teach me far more than human reason.
But faith, Lord, is your gift.
Pour it into my whole being in rich abundance.
May I live always in your presence.
May I always be able to say with Peter,
"Lord, it is good for me to be here" (Matt. 17,4).
May I never forget something else to-day's feast tells me,
that the presence of Moses, representing the Law,
and Elias representing the Prophets
demonstrates that the Law and the Prophets of the Old Testament
contemplate You, Lord Jesus, the Messiah, as their ultimate goal.
Make me, Lord, always a person of faith.
Help me to judge always, everywhere, all things
in the supernatural light of faith.
Give me your grace to live what I believe.

I think of you, my dear Mother. as the Church honours you.
Who can comprehend the dignity of your vocation?
Your Son was the "Blessed" one who came in the Lord's name.
You are "Blessed" among all women.
I think of you as you approached the end of your mortal course.
You were filled with divine love.
Further increase was impossible
as long as your soul was united with your body.
I see it leaping forth on its triumphant way to heaven.
How rapturous was your soul's first embrace with Jesus!
Did you speak loving words to Him like these?
"My Jesus, the body from which God took your Body is not here.
The bosom which nursed You so tenderly is on earth.
The hand that guided You,
the eyes that watched over You,
the lips that taught You and prayed with You,
the ears that loved to listen to You,
the Heart that loved You—
must they be allowed to corrupt in the earth?"
O Mother, I know it was not necessary for you so to pray.
I see your soul, escorted by angels,
rejoining your body where it lay.
Then, glorified, it ascended by the force of agility
to the throne of the divine God.
What a welcome awaited You!
All heaven had been waiting for this day,
the homecoming of the Queen.
Never had anything like this been experienced in heaven.
Well could the choirs of angels cry out:
"Who is she that cometh forth as the morning rising,
fair as the moon, bright as the sun
terrible as an army in battle array" (Cant. 6,3).
Mother I turn to you in your glory.
Side by side with your Son you pray.
united closely and indissolubly with Him.
You are God's Almoner, heaven's treasurer,
the channel of all graces.
I want to see you, my Mother, as God saw you.
I want to honour you as you deserve.
I want to consecrate myself to you,
to live in you always as Jesus did.

165 A MOTHER'S REWARD

O Mary, my Mother, I believe with all my heart
that when you had completed the course of your earthly life
you were assumed body and soul into the glory of heaven.
From all eternity you were joined in a hidden way with Jesus
in one and the same decree of predestination,
immaculate in your conception
a most perfect Virgin in your divine motherhood,
the noble associate of the divine Redeemer
Who has won a complete triumph over sin and its consequences.
You attained, as the supreme culmination of your privileges,
that you should be preserved free from the corruption of the tomb
and that like your own Son, having overcome death,
you were taken up, body and soul, to the glory of heaven,
where as Queen you sit in splendour at the right hand of your Son,
the immortal King of the Ages.
This privilege of yours, your Assumption into heaven, is fitting
because of the love and honour Jesus had for you,
because of your virginal divine Motherhood
because you were so completely united with your divine Son,
because He willed that of all his creatures you should be most like Him,
because you were united in the decree of your predestination,
because of your victory over sin and death,
because of your Immaculate Conception and freedom from sin,
because of the fullness of grace with which God endowed your soul,
because victory over death was befitting for you as the new Eve,
because of your marvellous personal perfection.
Yes, dear Mother, I believe that it is only reasonable and fitting
that not only the soul and body of a man,
but also the soul and body of a woman
should have obtained heavenly glory.
In heaven you are perfectly happy, glorified also in your body,
enjoying the vision of God and of the humanity of your Jesus,
being praised by the choirs of angels, being the happiness of the Saints
who contemplate you, unite themselves to your glory and praise you.
Dearest Mother, you are full of love and compassion for us.
You never cease to help us by your intercession.
Help our poor world to-day and every day
that our race will turn from sinful ways,
and embrace the truth revealed by your Son.

O Mary, Mother dear, how you rejoiced in peace
as the end of your pilgrimage on earth drew near.
Nothing could trouble the calm of your soul.
You never knew sin.
You used to perfection all the tremendous graces you received.
You accumulated merit upon merit.
Before the Lord all your days were full.
Not a moment was ever wasted.
You were never guilty of even an imperfect thought, word,
deed or omission.
Earth was for you a place of exile, an abode of captivity.
Jesus, the unique object of your love
had gone before you to the city of the angels and Saints.
You looked forward to joining Him there,
never to be separated from Him.
I think now of my life in contrast with yours.
Prepare me, dear Mother, for my last moment
by guiding me along the paths of fidelity and love.
You died of love.
The heavenly ardours which consumed you
caused you to experience an indescribable martyrdom.
I believe that your Immaculate Heart
could no longer bear up against their effects.
That divine fire consumed the ties which still bound you to earth
so that your beautiful soul gently separated itself from your body
and like a pure flame ascended to heaven.
I dare not try to imagine the delights which flooded your soul.
No mortal tongue can describe such bliss;
No human mind can fully comprehend it.
You trembled on the confines of the infinite.
But because I love you dearly
I dare to contemplate so far as I can its sweetness
and to rejoice at the beautitude which must have been yours.
How can I hope to congratulate you on your happy transit?
I do beg of you to obtain for me from the Sacred Heart of your Son
the grace to live so blessedly
that when He calls I shall have nothing to fear.
Obtain for me the grace never, never to lose sanctifying grace.
I wish to atone adequately for all my sins
and to grow in faith, hope, love and every virtue
every remaining day of my life.

167   QUEEN AND MOTHER

No human being was more like Jesus than you, O Mary.
You were like Him in everything.
Your love was like his love.
Your sufferings were in union with his.
At the end of your earthly pilgrimage
your Jesus magnificently and proportionately distinguished you
by making you even more like Himself
in the Kingdom of which He has taken possession.
He willed that you, my dearest Mother,
should abide in his glory and sovereignty.
He is King of all; you are Queen reigning with Him.
Exalted above all the Saints, your beloved children,
 you see at your feet all that is less than God.
 The choirs of angels pay you homage;
You are Queen of them all.
Once you proclaimed that the eternal Father
had paid attention to his handmaiden's humility.
In this you are like your dear Son.
He emptied Himself, becoming obedient even to death.
This humility and obedience were the causes of his glory.
So it is with you, my very own dear Mother.
In the path of humility you followed Him with absolute perfection.
I rejoice that we celebrate
your Assumption into his heavenly Kingdom.
There you reign to exercise a supremacy of mercy and clemency.
As Queen you dispose of all the treasures of your Son as you please.
Your desires are his desires.
You are always the Mother of mercy and love.
Your immense majesty does not alarm my weakness.
To the enemies of your Son,
to the powers of darkness and opponents of good,
you are indeed terrible as an army in battle array.
Protect me, your loving child.
Protect the Church, enrich it with heavenly gifts.
The Church is your child.
Strengthen her; give her more members;
give her leaders after your own Heart.
I offer you now my own love and veneration.
I consecrate myself again to Jesus through you,
all that I am, all that I have.
Obtain for me every virtue that is pleasing to the Heart of your Son.

O divine Essence, bottomless, boundless abyss of wonders.
O unfathomable ocean of greatness,
O Unity of my God,
O Simplicity,
O Eternity without beginning and without end,
to whom everything is continually present!
O Immensity, which fills all things and contains all things!
O Infinity, which embraces all imaginable perfections.
O Immutability,
O Immortality,
O inaccessable Splendour!
O incomprehensible Truth,
O abyss of Knowledge and Wisdom,
O Truth of my God,
O divine Power, creating and sustaining all things!
O divine Providence, governing all!
O Justice, O Goodness, O Mercy.
O Beauty, O Glory, O Fidelity!
O great God, in <u>You I adore</u>
all the grandeurs and perfections which I have been contemplating,
as well as all the immeasurable and inconceivable others
which are, and will remain, unknown to me.
I adore You.
I praise You.
I glorify You.
I love You for all that You are.
Oh! how my heart rejoices
to see You so great,
and so overflowing
with every kind of treasure and splendour!
Certainly if I had all these grandeurs
and You had none of them,
I would want to strip myself of them
and give them to You.
Now Jesus, I turn to You,
the same infinite God.
Your Sacred Heart is the symbol of your Love.
Longinus pierced You, Heart of limitless perfection.
Blood and water poured out
as You sacrificed Yourself for me.
How can I hope to return such love!

O mighty God, You are infinite Wisdom.
"He that shall find me shall find life" said the Wise Man (Prov. 8,35).
Wisdom, O God, is life.
Is not your wisdom queen and mother of all life?
Your wisdom is your love, for all in You is one.
Do I not know You. O God, by receiving wisdom in love?
Is it not your wisdom which brings about enlightened,
rapturous experience of You?
I long for wisdom to be my holy friend.
O divine Wisdom, I see You as the mother of creation.
From You spring the graces of being and of life.
Only through You can I view the mysterious features of the Creator
in the mirror of created values and orders.
O Wisdom, You are the gift of God.
Only by prayer can I obtain You as I desire.
You are the most precious of all goods.
The inspired poet of all rightly proclaimed,
"All good things come to me together with her" (Wisdom 9,11).
O how the inspired writers sang of You, symbol of the essence of God.
As the "mother of fair love" (Sir. 24,24)
You pour forth the rivers of life (ibid. 24,40).
You, O Wisdom of God, are creative truth.
Rooted in You are the divine ideas,
the eternal types of all being and becoming.
You are the mysterious unity of all the ideas of God.
You are created truth whose thoughts are things.
May I dare to contemplate You, O God, contemplating Yourself?
Simultaneously in Yourself You comprehend
with your eternal clear glance
the deepest source and origin of created things.
I bow in adoration, O God, of the riches of your thought.
Before me opens up an immense world which in You
is pure and spiritual and completely real.
I see every created thing,
as it is projected into the fluctuating region of the perishable,
carrying within itself an eternal mystery,
and finding its ultimate explanation
only in the eternal ideas which your love, O God, has conceived.
O eternal Wisdom, I love You, I adore You.

Lord God, I long to be holy.
I know this just cannot be unless
I love You, am sorry for my sins and reject the world.
Continue to enlighten me, O God, as to what is good and what is evil.
May I continue to grow in my knowledge
of your goodness and your beauty.
I want to love You much
and to discover more and more reasons for loving.
Make my soul ever more pure and cleansed of sin.
so that the rays of your divine light will be always more resplendent.
You, O God, are the true wisdom of the purified soul
for You wondrously illumine it with the ray of your light
and thus teach it all it needs to know to attain salvation.
My God, when I contemplate what You do for all your creatures
I am moved to beg even more for your help.
The beasts of the fields, the birds in the air, the fishes in the sea
seem to know by an instinct what is good for them and what is harmful.
You, Almighty Creator, gave them this instinct.
You taught the sheep which plants are harmful
and which are beneficial.
You inform the animals which creatures are their friends
and which their enemies.
How much more, O loving Father,
do you provide me with the knowledge I need
to preserve my spiritual life!
The works of grace are so much more excellent
and so much more above the powers of men.
Your word, O God, is loving and effectual
more piercing than any two-edged sword,
reaching into the division of the soul and the spirit
of the joints also and the marrow (Heb. 4,12).
Your knowledge destroys that evil union
in which the spirit is attached to the things of the flesh.
Teach me, Lord, everything that pertains to my salvation.
Teach me how great is the beauty of virtue the ugliness of vice,
the vanity of the world, the dignity of grace, the greatness of glory,
the sweetness and consolation of your Holy Spirit,
your own goodness, the devil's malice, life's brevity.
Lord, raise me high above the mountains,
where I can contemplate You in all your beauty.

171   WISE IN GOD

Give me the wisdom, God, to realise
how insignificant are all the things the world can give
or take away,
in comparison with what You can give to my soul.
In the words of Solomon, may I persevere in wisdom like the sun
and be not like the fool as changeable as the morn (Sir. 27,12).
By your gift of wisdom, Lord,
may I never be broken by fear.
May I not change when I gain power.
May I remain humble if I become prosperous.
May I not be smothered by adversity.
May I be always virtuous, constant and brave.
May I remain always the same, ever intent on You,
growing in virtue, ever nearer to You,
never fluctuating with the changes that occur in my life,
nor following every new doctrine,
nor falling for every new fashion,
nor experimenting with every gimmick,
but persevering in You,
established in charity,
firmly rooted in faith.
Lord, your wisdom is not of earth but of heaven.
It does not merely enlighten my intellect in a speculative way.
It moves my will,
it penetrates to the very depths of my heart.
What can be compared, O God, to the wisdom You give.
It is more precious then anything in the world,
more to be valued than all natural knowledge.
Your wisdom directs me to subject myself
to the directions and judgements of my superiors,
especially those with authority in the Church.
Wisdom repeats the words of Jesus,
"He who hears you, hears me" (Luke 10,16).
Your wisdom teaches me how I need the guidance of the Church.
In your loving Providence You give me both,
the gift of wisdom and the guidance of the Church
to supply for my weakness.
I know and believe that unless I follow humbly the doctrine and
guidance of the Church
I shall be unworthy of the inspirations and movements of grace.
So help me always, dear God

G

I contemplate You, my infinite eternal Father
as the God of life.
The life I received at baptism is rooted in your life.
It is the outpouring of your triune majesty.
It surges up eternally, divine, all powerful in You
one God, Father Son and Holy Spirit.
I know I am really too unworthy to know You,
to draw near to the mystery of your abounding life.
Yet You have revealed Yourself to us.
You did not wish your goodness to be unenjoyed
or your majesty unwitnessed.
Your life, O God, is knowledge and love—spirit life.
In You life does not subsist in one Person alone
but in three coequal Persons.
From all eternity, You, Father, knew Yourself.
You never began, You are the unoriginated.
In knowing Yourself You know all the glory of divine being and life.
This primal knowledge is so replete with your holy being,
so pure, so luminous, and sheerest actuality
that it posits a Second Divine Person.
O divine Father, the Son is your eternal countenance,
truly begotten from your infinite bosom.
What a wonderful, perfect mutual relation of self-giving
there is between You, eternal Father, only-begotten Son.
You, Son, gave Yourself wholly to your Father.
The divine love, issuing from You, Father and Son,
as from one heart,
can find its resting-point only in a Third Divine Person.
O Holy Spirit I adore You
who gather up in yourself all the vibrant rhythms of divine love.
You are the infinite life-breath of God.
You are the everlasting fire on God's altar.
You are the storm-wind of love.
You are the kiss of the Father and the Son,
the luminous bond of their union.
In your flaming ardour the orbit of the divine processions is ended.
You, Holy Spirit, are the pledge of the fellowship of Father and Son,
the sea and ocean of love.
As the reciprocal giving of Father and Son
You are the ultimate principle of all communicability of God to us.

173   ENDLESS FLOWERING

Divine Son of the Eternal Father
You are the brightness of his Glory,
and the figure of his substance (Heb. 1,3).
You are the Father's eternal countenance,
truly begotten, in beatific rapture, from the bosom of God.
In You the Father knows Himself,
wholly possesses Himself.
You proceed from the Father radiant with light
but You are even imminent in your origin.
You rest in the Father,
engulfed by the cherishing mystery of his embrace.
You proceed from the Father, true Son,
as the replica of the divine essence,
the endless flowering in his bosom,
the dayspring from on high
the dawn of God's youthful day,
the meridian of God's life,
begotten before the daystar,
walking in the splendour of his holy place (Ps. 109,3).
In you dwells the radiant majesty of God's life.
Now, wonder of wonders, before You O Lord, I profess my faith.
This same life which the Father is ceaselessly, timelessly,
forever communicating to You,
all this holy fullness which is yours by nature,
is by the free bounty of God
to overflow in grace into our souls.
Yes, dear Lord, as in a hushed sanctuary
the eternal Processions of You from the Father
and of the Holy Spirit from the Father and You
are enacted in the interior of my grace-filled spirit.
The morning star rises full of grace in my soul.
My privilege is to share in your eternal generation from your Father.
I believe it—the seed of God is planted in my soul
to mature towards God.
You, Son of God, by the necessity of your nature
radiate from the Father from all eternity.
Into the mysteries of this endless life stream I am lifted
only by a free act of divine overpowering love.
I have divine life, your life, in me.
I have been born of God.
I rest with You, the Only-begotten, in your Father's bosom.

My God, give me grace to grow in intimacy with You.
You have told me to call You Father.
I believe with all my being that You are limitless love.
Your essence is love.
Inflame me with the love which is your infinite self.
Draw me deep into your Son.
Your love begot your only eternal Son.
Your love created me.
Your love raised me to a new life.
You created me in that same one eternal love
with which You begot your Son
before all creation in the light of your morning.
Immerse me in this love.
Then I become a partaker of the outpouring of divine life
in the Holy Spirit.
By faith, hope and love may I reproduce
your eternal Processions within me.
By my faith I long to be caught up in Christ,
to be dead to myself, to be risen in Him.
Father, enliven my faith.
Make it a new organ of spiritual sight.
Make it grow until it becomes a suffusion with eternal light,
a created sharing of your eternal knowledge of Yourself,
an anticipation of the beatific vision,
the beginning of eternal life.
May I never cease, dear Father, to be enraptured
by the wonder-world of your infinite love, power and wisdom.
May my hope be an echo of that unbroken, joyous, secure
sense of triumph with which You possess Yourself.
Make my hope so bright and radiant
that I may rest more deeply in You.
May the power of my trust, dear Father, ripen out of love.
I believe that your gift of love
is a glowing and streaming forth
together with the eternal love-procession of the Holy Spirit.
Lord, Father, I long to live in a way shaped by faith, hope and love.
Protect your life within me with reverence,
Form me, dear Father; shape me to be as You will me to be.
Keep me ever soft and tractable, the work of your love.

Lord, through your Prophet You ask me,
"Be holy, because I the Lord your God, am holy" (Lev. 19,2).
To be holy I must imitate You as perfectly as I can.
This means that I must rid myself
of everything which is alien to your likeness, divine Master.
I know I cannot be divine
unless I first cease to be human,
that is unless I put aside as far as possible
the many imperfections and weaknesses of my human nature.
Yes, I know it only too well.
You call me to travel from self to You,
to lose everything in me that is repugnant to your divine holiness.
Only your grace can do that.
The inspired writer called it a consuming fire (Deut. 4,24)
because it consumes human depravity and imperfections.
Your grace, O God, draws all things to itself
to make them share in itself.
Lord, give me all the help I need to
mortify my own will,
avoid all sin,
control my passions,
free myself from excessive anxiety,
avoid too much attention to worldly affairs
and purify my intention in all the interests of my life,
spiritual and temporal.
Then Lord, your spirit will rule me.
I will always be disposed to approach You in love.
You will be ever ready to come to me through your grace.
What I want is to ignite my heart with the fire of love.
Teach me how to remove the obstacles to that fire.
I do not look for sweetness and consolation, Lord.
I desire to love not your consolations but You, for Yourself.
I know I cannot obtain true holiness
as long as the obstacles remain in me,
self-love, self-will and all the passions that flow from them.
I cannot conquer these obstacles, Lord,
unless You inspire, guide, help and strengthen me.
Inflame my whole being more and more.
Strengthen my longing. Keep it alive and vibrant.
Let me gaze on You, mighty Lord, and never cease to come to You.

ST. EDMUND ARROWSMITH

Great Saint, Martyr, Priest,
I pray to you to-day as I ponder your glorious death.
When the good Lord calls me,
may I have in my heart, if not in my hands as you had,
the two keys to heaven,
perfect love of God and true sorrow for my sins.
May my thoughts never stray far from my blessed Redeemer,
carrying his cross, being nailed to it and dying for me.
You, blessed Edmund, were filled with joy
as, lead to the hurdle, you contemplated your Master
sinking under the Cross.
You rejoiced to be judged worthy of ignominy for his name
and to be admitted to follow your Saviour's footsteps.
As you looked at what was prepared for your execution
you said that the mercy you looked for was in heaven
through the passion and death of our Saviour.
Dear Saint, pray for me that I may never forget this.
May I repeat as my death draws near, your prayer,
"I freely and willingly offer to thee, sweetest Jesus,
this my death in satisfaction for my sins"?
May I always be able to say with you to Jesus,
"I die for love of Thee,
for our holy Faith,
for the support of the authority of thy Vicar on earth,
the successor of St. Peter,
true head of the Catholic Church
which Thou hast founded and established".
I pray that when God calls me I shall be able to say as you did,
"I die a constant Roman Catholic;
and for Jesus Christ his sake . . .".
May my prayer for all around me be the same as yours,
"For Jesus, sake, have a care for your souls,
then which nothing is more precious".
And with you, Blessed Edmund, I say from my heart,
"Nothing grieves me so much as this England,
which I pray God soon to convert".
May I live always in the presence of the Saviour,
for whom you gave your life.
May I say continuously in my heart,
the prayer of your last breath,
"*Bone Jesu*, O good Jesus".

177 ABIDE IN MY LOVE

Jesus, I wish to abide, to live for ever,
without interruption in your love.
You are God.
Rightly therefore You command me to love You
with all my mind, with all my heart,
with all my soul, with all my strength.
The model You give me for my love
is nothing less than the loving union
between You and your heavenly Father.
Jesus, I wish to be united with You,
to abide in You in my mind.
Make my thoughts like your thoughts.
May I think like You.
You are the true light.
You enlighten every man who comes into this world (John 1,5).
My intelligence is a ray of light
which comes from You.
May it never stray from You.
Jesus, You already know that I long
for my will to be dominated by its attachment to your will.
I want to love You above all else.
I want to live, to rest in your love.
Yet I want to be active in drawing nearer to You.
I want to love You for all those who do not love You.
I want to love You for all those who to-day
as in your own day
"laugh You to scorn" (Matt. 9,24).
I want to love You
in reparation for all the sin in the world.
I want to love You
because You have first loved me.
I know that without You I am powerless.
Yet I want to give myself to You without reserve.
You want me to love You
as You love your Father.
Jesus, that is just what I want.
But without You I cannot grow in your love.
I feel so weak, so hopeless, so very sinful.
Strength me, my dear Jesus,
Teach me, guide me, direct me
how to abide always in your love.

Lord Jesus, You are the infinite God,
Lord and King of the whole universe.
You won the human race for Yourself
by sacrificing your life on the Cross.
Now, after nearly twenty centuries, so many millions know You not.
I dare not probe too deeply into the mystery
of why this should be.
Lord, You know how bitterly You suffered,
how You allowed your Precious Blood to pour from your wounds
that all men might be saved.
Why is it that so many millions are still not your followers?
Day after day, year after year, century after century,
thousands of Masses have been offered,
your infinite sacrifice continued,
yet your Church seems to make such slow progress.
False religions claim the fervent adherence of millions,
Christianity is torn by dissensions.
Too many of those who belong to the one Church You founded
seem to show so little fervour.
Why is it Lord? I do not know the answer.
Do You not accept all those Masses?
Are You displeased with your believing children?
Are we not praying enough, apostolic enough?
Even the efforts of your greatest Saints seem to produce fruit
that is negligiblle when compared to the world picture.
Tell me, dear Lord, is there anything more that I can do?
How can your Church lead to you
the millions who do not know You,
yet for whom You gave your life?
Your last words still ring out through the arches of the years
"Go into the whole world and preach the gospel to every creature"
(Mark 16,15).
Lord, pour the grace of insight into your believing children.
Fire them with the love which longs to share its treasures.
Give us Saints to lead us, to inspire us with zeal.
Fill your Church in every place in which it exists
with single-minded apostolic zeal.
Detach the thinking of those who believe in You
from all that is less important.
You can do it, Lord. Then for the sake of those for whom You died
fire your Church with zeal greater than ever in its history.

179   OUR LADY'S BIRTHDAY

O Mary, the day of your birth
was a turning point in the history of mankind.
It may be more correct to say that the turning point
had already occurred when you were conceived Immaculate.
How the choirs of angels must have rejoiced
to look from heaven and to see for the first time
a completely sinless baby girl.
You were always present to the eternal gaze of the infinite God
with Whom there is no past and no future.
Your child, the Church, triumphant, suffering and pilgrim,
this one Church celebrates your life to-day.
The souls of the Saints in heaven rejoice.
If this day had never been
if you had never been born
what would have happened,
is hidden in the mystery of the loving wisdom of God.
But it did happen.
You were born,
always destined to consent freely to become God's Mother,
to give the world Him
to whose sacrificial death all the human souls in heaven
owe their enjoyment of the beatific vision.
Likewise, our suffering brothers and sisters in Purgatory.
They know they are saved
through the Redeemer you gave to our race.
They know how you love them
and long for them to join you in heaven.
Dearest Mother, on this your feast, pray specially for them.
You know them all. They are your children.
Look, too, upon the pilgrim Church which honours you to-day.
Pray for all those who honour and pray to you with devotion.
Obtain for them the grace of true holiness.
The pilgrim Church needs Saints.
On this your birthday, pray to your Son
for all the pilgrims on earth.
"God wills every man to be saved" (I Tim. 2,4).
Pray your Son to bring them to Himself
as He alone knows how.
Pray for all sinners,
for those who have wounded your Immaculate Heart.
Pray that they will return to the fold of your Good Shepherd Son.

Dear Jesus, I think of You to-day
as I read the inspired words of St. Paul (Phil. 2,5).
He bids me have the same mind as You, infinite Lord.
I contemplate You.
Babe of Bethlehem,
Exile in Egypt,
Young Man and Worker in Nazareth,
Preacher and Miracle Worker.
You never had a beginning,
You always lived with the Father and the Holy Spirit,
the Second Person of the Blessed Trinity,
infinite in every perfection,
limitless immensity, love, goodness,
wisdom, power and beauty.
For love of us You did not cling to your divinity alone.
You emptied Yourself.
You took the form of a slave.
You became Man .
But that was not enough to satisfy your love.
You became obedient to the point of dying.
But even that was not enough.
You chose to die as a criminal on the Cross.
How can I ever hope to comprehend the full meaning of it all.
Infinite Being dying, nailed to a criminal's cross of shame.
I believe, dear Lord, that this is why You were exalted,
why You are King of kings and Lord of lords—
they made You a Victim of love.
I want to be the same, as St Paul required.
In my world I see your merciful love everywhere rejected.
Those on whom You wish to lavish it
scarcely think of You.
They devote themselves to serving creatures.
So little of their capacity to love is given to You.
Yet You gave your whole self for us.
Lord, raise up a great legion of victims of your merciful love,
and so find an outlet for the pent-up force of your infinite tenderness.
Jesus, grant me the happiness of being such a victim,
burnt up in the fire of your love.
I beg You to look down in mercy on a whole multitude of souls,
a whole legion of victims, so little as to be worthy of your love.

181   MOTHER OF SORROWS

My blessed Mother Mary, between You and Jesus
lived a most perfect union.
You were always indissolubly united in the closest possible way.
Whisper into my heart the secret of your sharing in his sufferings
I can only try to comprehend what union with your crucified Son
meant to you.
Your heart was filled to its capacity with divine love,
and its capacity for love was and still is
as great as even God can make it,
In spirit you died with your Jesus.
You were not said to be present in Gethsemane
or in the judgement hall
or when your Jesus was scourged and crowned with thorns
but you knew and saw all his sufferings beforehand.
When you told the angel that you were the handmaid of the Lord
you offered up your whole self with your Son.
In the very depths of your soul
you suffered with his most bitter sufferings.
Before your eyes, dear Mother, the divine sacrifice
for which you had borne and nurtured the Victim was finished.
How generously you offered to God's justice your own dearest Child.
Yes, in your Heart, stabbed by the sword of sorrow, you died with Him.
By means of this union you are the cause of our salvation.
If you had not given us your beloved Son to die in torment
we would not have been redeemed.
I can never thank you enough for giving yourself
as Mother and Mediatrix
and for offering your love and your maternal rights.
Never was a mother asked a sacrifice as difficult as yours.
You took part in the sacrifice of your divine Son on Calvary.
You gave to the world and nourished
the High Priest and priceless Victim.
More than all other creatures you completed the Passion of your Son.
Mother, pray that I may understand all that you have done for me.
Every thought, word and deed of your Son was of infinite value.
Your holiest, perfect thought, works and deeds were but finite.
But it was God's will that you should offer yourself
wholly and entirely, all you are, all you have,
in union with your Jesus.
Thus you completed the Passion of your Son for the Church.
I thank God for making you my Mother.
I thank you for receiving me as your child.

Inspired by your Holy Spirit, St. Paul tells me
to be always humble, gentle and patient.
When I remember the unworthiness of my life,
not only my sins, but even more, my failure to grow in virtue
I should surely be humble!
I pray, Lord, for a genuine sense of my unworthiness.
"Father, I have sinned against You.
I am no longer fit to be called your Son" (Luke 15,19).
O Jesus, You told me to learn from You
because You are meek and humble of heart.
I do wish to obey your behest. Help me dear Lord.
Help me, too, to grow in gentleness, mildness and tenderness.
I know, Lord, that this is your way.
Lead me always to treat others like I would treat You.
"As long as you do it to one of these my least brethren you did it to me"
(Matt. 25).
Give me patience, Lord, patience always with people!
but patience, too, in bearing trials without grumbling,
yet persevering in good.
"There is one body and one Spirit,
one hope, one Lord, one faith, one baptism,
one God and Father of all men" (Eph. 4, 4-6).
Yes, Lord, deepen my faith in the unity of your Church.
Protect your Church from those who misunderstand her unity.
After your Last Supper You prayed that your followers would be one
as You and your Father are one
so that the world would believe that He sent You (John 17,20 ff.).
Lord, could this prayer be rejected?
Is it possible that the Father could reject the very prayer
in which You stressed your unity with Him?
Lord, I believe that your priestly prayer was heard.
I believe, therefore, that unity is a quality, a mark
imprinted on the Church by your divine power.
Your Church must be united in essentials,
which means that all who believe in You
must believe the same truths,
must worship in the same essential way,
and must obey the same divinely appointed authority.
Yes, Lord, those who call themselves Christians are divided
but your Church never. She is always divinely one.

183   ST. VINCENT DE PAUL

Lord Jesus, to-day I think of St. Vincent de Paul.
I beg You to give me your grace to be like him.
May I always have and display mature wisdom.
May I ever be full of compassion and pity.
I wish to live always by firm faith.
Pour it, Lord, into the very depths of my soul.
Strengthen my hope.
Make it a firm anchor to support me.
You know, Lord, how intensely I long to be inflamed by perfect charity.
Like St. Vincent may I always live in holy fear of You, O my God,
and be truly upright and simple.
I long to be like You, dear Jesus, meek and humble of heart.
Give me your spirit to animate me,
to have me at all times generously maintain your glory,
Only You dear Lord, can saturate me with love
which, burning within me, will outwardly transport me
into zeal for souls.
Like St. Vincent may I find in Christlike poverty
the precious pearl and rich treasure of the Gospel.
May I be like the angels in my purity,
May I be faithful in obedience to your will
May I flee from the every appearance of evil.
May I sincerely aspire in all I do to the practice of perfect virtue,
May I be patient in suffering and indulgent in forgiving,
May I be invincible against the arrows of adversity.
May I grow in docility and obedience to the earthly Vicar of Christ.
May I be detached from all I possess and use all for your glory.
St. Vincent, I turn now to you.
Obtain for me fervour in prayer.
Pray that I shall worthily imitate the life and virtues of Jesus.
Pray that I shall persevere to the end of my life
in shunning evil and doing good.
Pray that I shall estimate everything by the standards of God.
May I rightly appreciate the Catholic priesthood
as a most precious treasure and gift of God.
Pray that I shall be able to preach the Gospel to the poor,
relieve the afflicted and console the miserable.
Pray for the Church that it will continue to be faithful,
the mystical Body of Christ,
loyal, fervent and filled with true zeal.

184 ST. MICHAEL

Merciful Father, to deliver your Church and your children
from all the enemies which surround us
send the prince of the heavenly hosts, blessed Michael.
To-day your Church is threatened probably more gravely
then ever before in its history.
The forces of materialism and irreligion are organised against it.
The fight is not against flesh and blood
but against the principalities and powers,
against evil spirits (Eph. 6,12).
I believe as I profess in reciting the Creed
that the holy angels are the special creations of your omnipotence.
When the inspired writers had glimpses of heavenly glory
they were unable in human words to describe what they saw
It is your will, O God, to use your angels
to help your human creations to attain salvation.
So I beg You, dear Lord, to call without delay on your angels
and especially blessed Michael,
to help us here on earth to overcome the powers of evil.
To-day your name and the holy name of Christ
are being blotted out of every level of life,
political, commercial, social, urban and family life.
Souls destined for eternal life
are being plundered and spiritually murdered.
The powers of darkness have so succeeded
that not one of your ten Commandments is widely obeyed.
So I beg You to listen to my very fervent prayer.
Commit blessed Michael to battle again.
He is filled with your wisdom;
he is the most powerful prince of your armies;
he is the splendour and fortress of the pilgrim militant Church;
he is the honour and joy of the Church triumphant.
Loving Father, we need his leadership now.
"Thy thousand thousand hosts are spread,
Embattled o'er the azure sky;
But Michael bears thy standard dread,
and lifts the mighty cross on high.
Grant us with Michael still, O Lord,
against the price of pride to fight;
so may a crown be our reward,
Before the Lamb's pure throne of light!"

185   OFFERING WITH ST. THERESE

O my God, O most blessed Trinity,
I desire to love You and to make You loved,
to work for the glory of your Church
by saving souls here on earth.
and by delivering those suffering in Purgatory.
I wish to fulfill perfectly your will,
and to reach the degree of glory You have prepared for me
in your Kingdom.
In a word, I wish to be holy.
but, knowing how helpless I am,
I beg You, my God, to be Yourself my holiness.
Since You have loved me so much
as to give me your only-begotten Son
to be my Saviour and my Brother,
the infinite treasures of his merits are mine.
I offer them gladly to You,
and I beg of You to look on me through the eyes of Jesus,
and in his Heart aflame with love.
Moreover, I offer all the merits of the Saints in heaven and on earth,
together with their acts of love and those of the holy angels.
Lastly, I offer You, O Blessed Trinity,
the love and merits of the Blessed Virgin, my dear Mother;
to her I commit this oblation, praying her to present it to You.
During the days of his life on earth her Son, my beloved Brother,
spoke these words: "If you ask the Father anything in my name,
He will give it to You" (John 16,23).
Therefore I am certain You will grant my prayer.
O my God, I know that the more You wish to bestow
the more You make us desire.
In my heart I feel boundless desires
and I confidently beg You to take possession of my soul.
I cannot receive You in Holy Communion as often as I would wish,
but are You not all powerful?
Abide in me as You do in the tabernacle.
never abandon your little victim.
I long to console You for ungrateful sinners,
and I implore You to take from me liberty to cause You displeasure.
If through weakness I should chance to fall,
may a glance from your eyes straightaway cleanse my soul
and consume all my imperfections,
as fire transforms all things into itself.

I thank You, O my God,
for all the graces you have granted me,
especially for having purified me in the crucible of suffering.
At the day of judgement I shall gaze with joy upon You
carrying the sceptre of the Cross.
And once You have deigned to give me the precious cross
as my portion
I hope to be like You in Paradise,
and to behold the sacred wounds of your Passion
shine in my glorified body.
After earth's exile I hope to possess You eternally
but I do not seek to lay up treasures in heaven.
I wish to labour for your love alone—
with the sole aim of pleasing You,
of consoling Your Sacred Heart
and of saving souls who will love You through eternity.
When the evening of life comes
I shall stand before You with empty hands
because I do not ask You, my God, to take account of my works.
All our good deeds are blemished in your eyes.
I wish therefore to be robed with your own justice
and to receive from your love the everlasting gift of Yourself.
I desire no other throne, no other crown but You, O my beloved.
In your sight time is nought—
one day is a thousand years (Ps. 39,4).
You can in a single instant prepare me to appear before You.
In order that my life may be one act of perfect love,
I offer myself as a holocaust to your Merciful love,
imploring You to consume me unceasingly
and to allow the floods of infinite tenderness gathered up in You
to overflow into my soul,
that I may become a martyr of your love, O my God.
May this martyrdom one day release me from my earthly prison,
after having prepared me to appear before you
and may my soul take its flight
—without delay—
into the eternal embrace of your merciful love.
O my Beloved, I desire at every beat of my heart
to renew this oblation an infinite number of times
till the shadows retire, (Cant. 4,6)
and everlastingly I can tell You my love face to face.

187 WITH ST. FRANCIS

Lord Jesus, I contemplate the life of St Francis of Assisi.
I beg for just a little of his spirit of seraphic love.
Give me grace to love You above and before all else.
The world around me makes itaelf so compelling, so attractive.
But, Lord, men can only make scientific progress,
they can advance in technology,
only by knowledge and wisdom that come from You.
Francis denied himself, mortified his flesh,
simply because he wanted to love You above all.
He wanted to be like You in everything.
He longed to resemble You in the ecstasy of Thabor
but he wished to walk your way also to Calvary.
In his flesh he bore the marks of your wounds.
Dear Lord, I know that is impossible for me,
but at least I can and do offer in union with your sufferings
all the trials, difficulties, frustrations, anxieties and disappointments
of my life.
Lord, Francis learned from You to be meek and humble of heart.
He was one of those little ones
to whom your Eternal Father revealed sublime truth.
May I imitate him also in this.
Lord, I see around me
too many who seem to wish to set aside your Church.
May I love and serve your Church
in reparation for all those who do not love her as they should.
Francis tried to go afar to preach your truth to the pagans.
Give me something of his zeal.
Teach me how to influence all whom I meet
so as to lead them to You.
Give me the tact and the courage to be an effective apostle.
Yes, Lord, You need your champions to-day.
I know I am unworthy of such an honour.
But that is my sincere longing—
to be one of your champions,
to confound those who deny your truth,
to convert the pagans who worship only this world.
Lord give me the simplicity of Francis.
Give me your grace so that I shall be able to influence those I meet.
Remove from me anything which repels others.

Holy Spirit, I thank you for the holy Rosary.
Only your divine wisdom could have devised
such a simple, effective way of encouraging us
to consider the mystery of Redemption.
I thank You, also, for the blessings
which have come to your people through the Rosary.
I believe, with the Vicar of your Son, Pope Clement XIII,
that the victory of Lepanto was due to the recitation of the Rosary.
I believe, too, that Pope Clement XI was right
in attributing the victory of Prince Eugene at Peterwardem
to the power of the Rosary.
Dear Mother Mary, I thank you, too.
for appearing with your Rosary at Lourdes,
I thank you especially for coming to three children at Fatima
and asking them to tell the world
of your desire that the Rosary be recited.
Lord Jesus, send a shower, a veritable torrent, of grace
on your Church so that the Rosary
will be used and appreciated as much as God wishes.
You must will men to understand and appreciate
the mystery of your Incarnation and Redemption.
Move more of your children not only to say the Rosary
but to use it as a way of meditating
on the highest points of all history of earth and heaven.
Enlighten their minds to see in the Rosary
a wonderful, as it were, conducted tour
by your own Mother of the fifteen chosen mysteries.
Arouse interest in the Rosary. Cause more people to understand it.
Let them see how delightful and beneficial it is
to contemplate the Annunciation, the Visitation,
Bethlehem, Gethsemane, Calvary,
your Resurrection and Ascension,
the birthday of your Church,
your Mother's Assumption into heaven,
her crowning
and the glory of the multitude of your Saints,
side by side with Mary, under her direct care,
present with her at each mystery.
What a privilege to try to see with her eyes hear with her ears,
understand with her mind and love with her heart
these marvellous manifestations of your love.

189   THE MIRACLE OF THE SUN

My dear Lord, I talk with You to-day
about what is called the miracle of the sun.
It happened on this day in 1917.
Yes, Lord, I thank You for this evidence
that your blessed Mother had indeed appeared at Fatima.
She, your most magnificent creation ,
appeared to ask a simple child for the Rosary.
Lord, I ponder within myself—why the Rosary?
In those fifteen mysteries we contemplate
the most important events in the history of angels or of men.
I imagine myself taken by the hand by your lovely majestic Mother,
She bids me contemplate Archangel Gabriel
proposing your Incarnation to her.
You, infinite in all your attributes,
infinite Being, love, power, beauty, goodness, wisdom, immensity,
rest in her virginal womb.
Now she bids me behold her journey to Elizabeth
carrying You, infinite God, to sanctify him who was to go before You.
Then to Bethlehem, to hear the angels You created
herald your coming and proclaim your message of peace.
To your own Temple then, Lord, as You are offered
and as You mysteriously will to be lost.
She leads me next to Gethsemane
to adore You, immense God, sweating blood,
to the yard of your scourging, crowning and mockery.
She bids me see You there as the God of all creation,
the God who created all that scientists know.
who made all the laws they discover.
With her I adore You on the way to Calvary
and dying, nailed to the Cross.
She takes me to see You rise in triumph on Easter morn.
and to rise beyond the clouds from the mount of Olives.
Next to the Cenacle and those mysterious tongues of fire,
the Holy Spirit one and the same God as Yourself.
Yes, Lord, with your Immaculate Virgin Mother I see it now.
Fifteen mysterious events impregnated with the divine.
You and your Mother bid me contemplate them
and gather their full significance.
That is the way to intense faith and fervent love.
Thank You, dear Lord, for teaching me this precious truth.

My God, I thank you to-day for St. Teresa
and all she has meant to the Church.
I beg You to give me your grace to be zealous
for your glory and the life of prayer.
Send from heaven mighty graces to inspire us
to realise that to love You is our first duty.
Lord, may the spirit of adoring love grow in your Church.
I believe that people do not pray
because they do not contemplate You
nor realise the meaning of your infinite perfections,
Send a mighty wave of your inspiring grace
so that a new movement of devoted contemplative prayer
will penetrate and saturate Your Church
Raise up zealous servants devoted to You
who with strength of mind like Teresa
will spread around them deep conviction
and new comprehension of your infinite reality.
May they display for all an example
of true detachment from the things of earth.
Lord, stem the stream of materialism and pleasure-seeking
which is drawing souls ever away from You.
Inspire your children to get their priorities right,
to put your love before every other love,
eternity before time,
holiness before enjoyment,
service of others before selfishness,
abandonment to your will before wordly ambition,
zeal for the Church before every other enthusiasm.
Lord, help us all, and especially my own poor self
to desire as You do the salvation of souls.
Help me to taste and see how sweet You are
as we pass through this vale of tears.
When those around me those dear to me die,
may I be reminded that death must not be feared
but loved as the way to true life.
Lord, make me love the Cross of Christ.
Help me to see it in all my pains, troubles and anxieties.
You filled St Teresa with the treasures of your love,
May I love You and suffer all that is painful
for You and in union with You.

191   DRAW NEAR TO THE THRONE OF GRACE

O God, how inexhaustible is the meaning of your Incarnation!
You became man because You love us.
Your love brought each of us out of nothing.
You could have created others instead of me.
But You chose me.
You could have made one whom You knew would be a great Saint.
But You chose me.
You destine me to live in heaven with You for ever.
How can I ever repay You, O Lord,
for the myriad things You have done for me?
You gave us a High Priest who can sympathise with our weakness,
one who has been tempted as we are.
Yes, I marvel that God the Son
allowed Himself to be tempted in the desert
and all through his earthly life suffered difficulties,
and in his public life especially
because of the opposition of the Scribes and Pharisees.
All this was proof of your merciful love, O Lord,
You gave us your own divine Son to be our leader
and our intermediary between Yourself and us.
O my God, I know deep down in my heart
that the real purpose of this life is eternal happiness.
Lord make me realise more vividly
that my life here on earth is but a preparation for the real life to come.
Make me remember that I have a divine Brother, Jesus Christ,
who is pleading for me at the throne of grace.
Oh how lacking I am in courage and confidence.
I allow myself to be downcast by thoughts of this world.
O my Jesus, I turn to You.
You know my weaknesses and my temptations.
You know how often and how seriously I have sinned.
I am sorry, Lord.
Please obtain from my Father in heaven the pardon I long for.
I thank You for going before me to prepare a place for me in heaven.
What a mystery is here—
that You the one infinite Being, limitless in all your perfections
should love me, a poor creature, so much
that You died for me, so that You can share heaven with me.
With such an intermediary and helper,
how can I fail to reach eternal joy?
Lord be with me. Help me always.

Lord, deep down in my heart I am disturbed
by what is happening in your Church to-day.
I believe that You must permit the trials which affect your Church.
You foretold that she would always be persecuted and hated,
just as You were persecuted and hated
not because You were bad but because You were good.
Even among those You, all knowing God, chose to be your Apostles
one denied You, one betrayed You and most of them deserted You.
I am distressed to see so many of those who claim to be scholars
raising doubts and disturbing the minds of simple people
about such fundamental doctrines as
original sin, your Virgin-birth, the events of your infancy,
your real, true Eucharistic presence,
the infallibility and supremacy of your Vicar on earth
and many of your revealed teachings on moral conduct.
Everything is present to your eternal gaze.
In your love and goodness
you permitted the visible shepherd of your flock, Pope John XXIII,
to call the second Vatican Council.
Lord, I know that the Council was guided by your Holy Spirit.
Yet it has been followed by years of disturbance
caused by the dissent and publicised doubts of the theologians
whose true vocation is to guide and help your bishops.
What distresses me, Lord, is that this turbulence
seems to have deprived the Church of her sense of mission.
I recall your own prayer to your Father,
"I thank You Lord, God of heaven and earth,
for hiding these things from the wise and learned
and revealing them to little ones!" (Matt. 11,25).
Dearest Jesus, am I wrong in sensing that
this absence of visible apostolic zeal
is the cause of the dearth of vocations
to the priesthood and the religious life?
Lord, I beg You bring turbulence and dissent to an end.
The Church is your other self, your mystical Body.
Restore the sense of mission.
Move bishops and priests everywhere to accept, love and act upon
the directives of the second Vatican Council
that in every place the Church must be and be seen to be
a body at whose heart lies the sense of mission,
then out of the evil of dissent will come a renewal of apostolic zeal.

193 ENGLAND

Lord, this land in which I was born,
where I have always lived
was once the Dowry of your Mother
and an island of Saints.
Now it seems to be a cauldron of irreligion.
Your commandments are no longer observed by the majority.
I long to make reparation to You
for the way in which my country has turned from You.
I want to console your Sacred Heart for the lack of fervour,
the indifference, coldness and lukewarmness
of so many members of your Church.
I remember my joy at the Mass of your Vicar on earth
when on this day in 1970 he proclaimed
that forty glorious men and women are indeed martyrs
and reigning with their souls in heaven.
But Lord, this people is falling far from You.
When this was a poor little obscure Kingdom
hardly known by the great nations of the world
You created here your Saints.
You were pleased by the great knowledge of the truth,
the devotedness and the love of the Sacraments of your people.
But now, when my country is regarded
as one of the leading nations of the world
You are forgotten, ignored, even despised.
Listen, Lord, to the prayers of the souls
of our English Saints and Martyrs.
Replace our national apostasy by a national return to You.
I pray to You, Lord, as your servant John Henry Newman prayed:
"O look not upon our haughtiness and pride;
look not upon our contempt of truths invisible;
look not upon our impurity;
but look upon your own merits,
look upon the wounds in your hands;
look upon your past mercies towards us;
and, in spite of our wilfulness,
subdue our hearts to You, O Saviour of men,
and renew your work in the midst of the years,
in the midst of the years re-establish it."
Jesus, convert England.
Jesus, have mercy on this country.

Dear Jesus, You are my God and my all.
During my life I have allowed myself to be wounded by my sins.
I am still so proud and vain, so self-centred and self-willed,
so prone to be tempted to impurity and lustful thinking.
I believe that You, Lord, are the infinitely wise and good
Physician of souls.
Heal me in your love.
Lord, I burn with anger at what I see around me.
Sometimes red-hot passion surges up within me.
Prince of peace and tranquillity
be for me always a cooling, refreshing fountain.
Lord, as I look back over the years I have lived
I feel weighed down with iniquity.
You know exactly when I have been virtuous
and when I have been wicked.
You know the degree of my guilt.
I trust in your infinite justice.
Lord, I am so very weak.
The devil, the world and the flesh attract and attack me.
I am so weak that I fear I shall fall from Your grace.
Lord, be with me always.
Be my strength.
O Jesus, I fear the death of sin.
I fear that my life may end when I am dead to You.
Be always my life.
Guide me, protect me, lead me.
Go before me so that the shadows will be behind me.
Yes, Lord, You know how I long for heaven.
I believe that You are the Way.
But, Lord, are You the narrow, winding, hilly Way?
Take me by the hand.
Carry me in your arms until You call me.
Lord, my faith, my spirit, my soul
need divine food.
I know You are that food.
You said that those who eat You
live by You.
Let that be me, dear Lord.
Feed me always.
Every day I long to taste and see
how infinitely sweet you are.

195   DEATH—NEW BIRTH

Dearest Father, mighty God, loving Providence,
You will that we should always be reminded of death.
Not a day, hardly an hour goes by without some reminder.
How kind You are!
The moment of death is the most important moment of life.
I believe that my life for a timeless eternity
depends on the state of my soul at that moment.
I believe, too, that in preparing for that moment
I depend entirely on You.
I cannot take a step towards sanctity or salvation
without your grace.
My thoughts of death now as I pray
are your gift to me.
Continue to help me, good Father.
I want to live always as your loving child.
I am sorry for all the times I have offended You.
I offer up all my trials, frustrations, anxieties,
work, pain, embarrassments in reparation for my sins.
Lord, strengthen my desire for the new life of heaven.
Here You enable me to live.
You give me food and drink to consume,
air to breathe and sleep to restore.
But, Lord, what are these to the happiness of heaven.
No eye has seen,
no ear has heard
no mind has conceived
all that You have prepared for your lovers.
Make me always one of those.
I depend on You to increase my capacity to love.
I live now.
At a moment which You alone now know
I am to be born again.
In my new life I hope to see You as You are,
Three in One, limitless in love and beauty and every perfection.
I look forward to meeting the Queen of eternal life,
my Mother Mary who I know so lovingly desires my salvation.
I try to contemplate the countless choirs of the angels,
the thousands of souls of the blessed.
Lord, enlighten my whole being to live to be born again.

Lord Jesus, to-day I pray with You after your last Supper.
Then You prayed, "I do not pray for these only, but also
for those who believe in me through their word" (John 17,20).
I believe, O Jesus, that because You are God
your prayer must be infallibly effective.
O, enlighten the minds of all your followers
that they may see that this is so.
Your prayer convinces me that there will always be
only one true Church.
Unity is an essential property of your Church.
Lord, sincere ecumenists are searching for unity. It exists already.
The Church You founded is "indefectably one in faith, in worship
and in the bond of hierarchical communion".
So proclaimed your Vicar on earth, Paul VI.
As You were preparing to suffer for us You revealed
what the foundation of the unity of your Church would be.
You told us what effects follow from it. I thank You.
How infinitely generous You were to reveal in your prayer
and to have your beloved Apostle record it,
that the source from which the mark of unity flows
is the intimate unity between You, the Father and the Holy Spirit.
Among You in the Holy Trinity there is mutual love and self-giving.
Lord, your holy Church proclaimed—may I deeply understand it—
"The Lord Jesus, when praying to the Father
'that they may all be one . . . . even as we are one'
has opened up new horizons closed to human reason
by implying that there is a certain parallel
between the union existing among the divine persons
and the union of the sons of God in truth and love.
It follows, then, that if man is the only creature on earth
that God has wanted for its own sake,
man can fully discover his true self
only in a sincere giving of himself" (*Gaudium et spes*, 24).
O Lord, I believe this with all my heart.
I believe, too, that the unity of the Church You founded
is also grounded on the union of believers with You
and through You with the Father.
O Lord, enlighten all who seek and work for unity
to grasp the truth that its fullness is attained only through the grace
which comes to us through You.

197   CHRIST PRAYS FOR UNITY

Lord Jesus, I contemplate your own prayer.
You said You prayed "for those
who believe in me through their word,
that they may all be one,
even as thou, Father, art in me,
and I in thee,
that they also may be in us,
so that the world may believe
that thou hast sent me" (John 17,21).
Yes, Lord, it is through union with You
that we in your Church are united among ourselves.
O grant that those everywhere who sincerely seek the truth
will be moved to see the unique unity of your Church,
and to see it as a sign raised up for the nations to see,
inviting all to believe that You are sent by God to save all.
Lord, move your children to understand how your Church
carries on the mission of salvation through her union with You
calling all mankind to join her
and by so doing to share in union with You and with the Father.
Dear Lord, You well know how I desire true unity,
the unity as You express in your prayer to your Father.
You expressed your desire for unity through prayer.
Move all who believe in You
to pray for true unity, the unity for which You prayed.
How moving are your words as I read them now.
"The glory which thou hast given me
I have given to them,
that they may be one even as we are one,
I in thee and thou in me,
that they may become perfectly one" (John 17, 22-23).
Lord Jesus, You possess glory, a manifestation of divinity
because You are God, equal to the Father.
How can I thank You for giving your disciples this glory.
Indeed, You make us partakers of the divine nature (2 Peter 1,4).
By your grace You make us ever more like You.
You, dear Jesus, are the likeness of the Father (2 Cor. 4,4).
I thank You for joining us to God
by communicating your glory,
giving us nothing less than a share in supernatural life.
Am I wrong, my Lord, in believing that this
is the source of the holiness of those who believe in You
and of your Church?

"Father, I desire that they also
whom thou hast given me,
may be with me where I am,
to behold my glory which thou hast given me
in thy love for me before the foundation of the world" (John 17,25).
O my dear Lord, I thank You for your priestly prayer.
I thank You for having your beloved disciple transmit it to us.
I thank You for revealing to us
that your eternal Father's revelation of himself through You
causes us to begin to share in the divine life,
a sharing which will reach its climax in heaven.
I recall the words of your Vicar on earth, Paul VI,
who proclaimed our belief that only God, God alone,
can give us right and full knowledge
of the reality of supernatural life
by revealing Himself
as Father, Son and Holy Spirit.
I thank You, dear Lord, for your redeeming death
which makes possible our sharing by grace
in the eternal life of the Blessed Trinity.
Yes, Lord, I recognise the obscurity of faith.
I look forward to the eternal light
that I hope will be mine when You call me to Yourself.
O Jesus, I thank You for your immense love
in revealing to us all we need to know
in order to participate in the mutual love of the divine Persons.
Lord, You have revealed to us the mystery of who You are
and what your mission is.
You prayed, "I have made known to them thy name,
and I will make it known
that the love with which thou hast loved me
may be in them,
and I in them" (John 17,26).
Yes, Lord, you have revealed to us the mystery of God Himself.
In this way You fulfilled what You had announced,
"No one knows the Father except the Son
and any one to whom the Son chooses to reveal him" (Matt. 11,27).
O dear Lord, why do so many remain ignorant of these truths?
You continue to make known your Father's love,
by means of the Church in which You are always present.
Lord, how can I thank You for the gift of faith?

199   CHRIST THE KING

O my Jesus, I bow down before You.
You are the one King of All.
I believe with all my being that You are God,
the one infinite Being, who created everything outside Yourself.
"Without You was not anything made that was made" (John 1,3).
Along with the Father and the Holy Spirit, You, Lord, are an active
principle of creation.
I believe that the work of creation is an activity
common to the three divine Persons of the Blessed Trinity.
I profess my faith again in the eternal Father generating,
You, Lord, the Son being born, the Holy Spirit proceeding,
consubstantial, co-equal, co-omnipotent, co-eternal;
one origin of all things;
the Creator of all things, visible and invisible,
spiritual and corporeal.
You, Lord Jesus, are indeed King
by right of being the God and Creator of all things.
You are King, too, because You became man
and stand forth the first and greatest of men.
You are King because You redeemed our race
and this obligated all men to Yourself.
You are King because of your infinite goodness and kindness
with which in such a singular way You reach out
to all mankind, notably in the Mystery of your Love.
You alone, divine Jesus, were able to save us from Satan's power.
You alone are able to conquer
the injustice, the selfishness and all the misery of our world.
You alone are able to establish peace and justice on our poor earth.
Do it, O Lord, by your mighty loving power.
You have satisfied divine Justice infinitely more
than all the victims of the Old Testament put together.
Why, then, does sin still reign?
Why do those for whom You died still laugh You to scorn?
Why are so few of them fervent in their love for You?
Why are your commandments so ignored?
Lord, is it merely because of the ignorance and perversity of men?
Can your omnipotence not move them to turn to You?
Does your infinite love not move You to enlighten them?
O what a mystery, dear Jesus,
is this universal rejection of your Kingship.
Give me love and faith to be ever loyal.

My dearest Mother, I turn to you to-day.
We celebrate your self-giving to God.
Immaculate, you must from your earliest years
have surrendered yourself completely to his will.
Your years in the Temple prepared you for the great moment.
God's messenger was a party with you
at the greatest peace conference ever held.
When Gabriel, in answer to your humble enquiry,
explained how you were to become a mother
without surrendering your virginity
you uttered those memorable words of surrender,
"Behold the handmaid of the Lord;
be it done to me according to your word" (Luke 1,38).
The Eternal Word, God the Son, your Creator
began to live in you.
So to that free consent of yours
we owe all that the coming of Christ has meant to the world.
As the Word was made flesh
and dwelt amongst us
God the Son was ordained the great High Priest
whose sacrifice was to redeem the world.
Your "Magnificat" is a song of
loving acceptance of God's will.
At Cana you gave us a formula for living,
"Whatsoever He says to you, do it" (John 2,5).
O Mother, obtain for me grace
to live always in perfect, loving abandonment to God's will.
Because you chose God's will above all else
you became his mother.
Your consent had been in his mind for an eternity.
How blessed you are for giving the free consent
which brought Him to live in you
who created you for this moment.
I see the mystery continued in the Church.
You are a member of the Church.
You are mother of the Church.
The Church is the Body of your Son.
So as He chose to live in you
He wills the Church to live in you
so that you will bring all its members
to birth in the fullness of Christ.

201 SHARING IN GOD

O God, I can never thank You as I ought.
Your divine power has given me everything I need
to be a Saint.
You have called me to share your own glory and goodness.
What a wonderful gift!
What unsurpassable generosity!
You not only call me, O loving Father;
You give me all the helps I need.
Indeed the gifts You give me are great and precious.
Only by faith can I understand them.
And faith is your gift, too.
Not only do You show me how to escape from the lusts of the world.
You call me to share in your very own nature (2 Peter 1,4).
For a timeless eternity your nature has been to know and love.
You endow me with supernatural life,
sanctifying grace,
which is a created miniature of your divine nature
by which I am able to know You in the way You know Yourself
and to love You in the way You love Yourself.
Yes Lord, I shall try to add goodness to my faith.
To my goodness I shall try to add understanding.
To my understanding I shall try to add self-control.
Only with your assistance can I make progress, dear Father.
Enable me to add to self-control endurance.
To my endurance help me to add godliness,
imitating your own perfection.
I long to be perfect according to the capacity You give me.
Empower me to add to my absorption in You
the practice of brotherly love.
To my love of men may I add even more love of You.
Yes, guide me, help me
to make your call and your choice of me
a permanent experience.
Grant that I may never fall away;
I believe that with your ever present help
I will be given the full right
to enter the eternal Kingdom
of my Lord and Saviour, Jesus Christ.

Lightning Source UK Ltd.
Milton Keynes UK
UKOW01f2035190117
292462UK00001B/1/P